The Concise Guide to Minimalism

Remove the Noise in Your Life, Organize Your Surroundings and Live Happier by Becoming a Minimalist.

Josh Parker and Dan Harris

© **Copyright Josh Parker - All rights reserved.**

The content contained within this book may not be reproduced, duplicated or transmitted without direct written permission from the author or the publisher.

Under no circumstances will any blame or legal responsibility be held against the publisher, or author, for any damages, reparation, or monetary loss due to the information contained within this book, either directly or indirectly.

Legal Notice:

This book is copyright protected. It is only for personal use. You cannot amend, distribute, sell, use, quote or paraphrase any part, or the content within this book, without the consent of the author or publisher.

Disclaimer Notice:

Please note the information contained within this document is for educational and entertainment purposes only. All effort has been executed to present accurate, up to date, reliable, complete information. No warranties of any kind are declared or implied. Readers acknowledge that the author is not engaged in the rendering of legal, financial, medical or professional advice. The content within this book has been derived from various sources. Please consult a licensed professional before attempting any techniques outlined in this book.

By reading this document, the reader agrees that under no circumstances is the author responsible for any losses, direct or indirect, that are incurred as a result of the use of the information contained within this document, including, but not limited to, errors, omissions, or inaccuracies.

Table of Contents

Introduction 8

Chapter 1: What is Minimalism? 14
   Minimalism Through The Ages 19
      Minimalism as a Philosophy 28

Chapter 2: Why Should You Declutter? 33
   How Does Living With Less Make You Happier? 41

Chapter 3: How Do You Make Minimalism Part of Your Life and Not Just Your Space? 45
   Mind, Body, Soul, and Space 46
      Digital Decluttering 52

Chapter 4: How to Organize Your Space 57
      Organizing Your Space 64

Chapter 5: How to Stay Clutter-Free 75
   Managing a Relapse 82

Chapter 6: How Not to Do Minimalism 87
   Is That Minimalism? 95

Chapter 7: How Does Minimalism Help The Environment? 98

What Else Can You Do to Help?..........................103

Conclusion..*110*

References..*115*

Introduction

Figure 1: An Empty House

You are probably a little skeptical. I know what you have heard and no, I am not going to make you throw out all of your belongings. You also won't have to live in a bare-faced house with white walls and white furniture and two obscure little cube decorations. Like many things in life, minimalism is a choice, and if you are going to implement it into your life, then you have to be committed. I'm not going to preach to you about the fundamental principles of minimalism and how to follow them to the letter because, in the end, minimalism can be a very subjective concept. Many "true minimalists" out there might tell you that you are doing it wrong. "Minimalism is about depriving yourself!" They'll protest, waving their perfectly square placards through the air of their perfectly empty homes. Don't listen to them.

Minimalism is going to take you on a journey of truth and freedom. Throughout the many lives and interpretations of minimalism, one thing has remained constant and that is that minimalism is not only a concept or set of rules but a philosophy. Your journey may not always be easy but the rewards will be so satisfying. By interpreting minimalism as a philosophy, we allow it to permeate through our lives. Throughout this book, I will show you how to fully integrate minimalism into your life and space. The question remains, how does decluttering benefit you? Well, dear reader, we aren't only going to be decluttering. We are going to change your life! I will help you implement the simple practice of minimalism into your home, your mind, your social life, your work calendar, your phone and so much more.

But before I start changing your life, we are going to have to explore what minimalism is, why it is and how it is. One of the most bizarre aspects of minimalism is that it is everywhere! You can find minimalism in language, architecture, programming, design, furniture, art and even politics. Almost every single subject and niche has its own form of minimalism. This speaks so clearly to the human condition, especially in an economically and environmentally vulnerable time. Our lives are messy, we are busy, we have too much work to do, too many friends to see and when the day is finally over and all we want to do is relax; we walk through a door that leads us to another cluttered room. It's no wonder humans are trying to find ways to merely survive in this world without feeling claustrophobic.

Minimalism, through the ages, has been many things. Some people will think of minimalism as a process of discarding until you are left with nearly nothing. For the Zen Buddhists, it was a way to create space for self-realization. For the Bauhaus movement, it embodied functionality and form. For minimalist artists, it was a counter-response to traditional art. For programmers and scientists, minimalism is a way to create understandable and simple equations and algorithms. While these interpretations are all somewhat different, a holistic exploration of minimalism calls us to refer back to all of them. In this book, we will look at minimalism through all of these lenses; as a process to self-actualization, a simplification of structure, a usefulness and usability, and a response to wasteful and claustrophobic living. Engaging with all of these various dogmas means that we can understand minimalism in its entirety and therefore appreciate it for what it truly represents.

Minimalism, therefore, is not just about owning less, it is about creating space in your life. If your schedule is constantly full and you are endlessly buying new things and moving through life without any real consideration, then how can you possibly have any space for yourself or the things that really matter to you? By living a minimalist lifestyle and being intentional with your time, space and heart, you give yourself time to process, heal and focus. In the upcoming chapters, I will provide you with a set of tips, tricks and strategies for living your best minimalist life. Many other gurus will provide you with one 'full-proof' method that they swear by, but people are different and one style of minimalism may suit some people and not others. You may want to try the 90/90 method (Millburn & Nicodemus, 2020), or perhaps sort room by room (Becker, 2019). You may even want to sort through your home as life takes you, no pressure, no structure. The goal is to allow people to find their own way of interacting and integrating with minimalism, otherwise the process can feel forced and arbitrary. Don't feel like you need to reign yourself in or force yourself to be someone you're not. Find a method that works for you. Remember, if done right, minimalism is freeing, not limiting. So, if the minimalist shoe doesn't fit, try on another one!

Besides advising you on which minimalist style will best suit you and how to downsize your space, this book will guide you and create a space for you to set some much-needed boundaries between you and this world. Don't worry, boundaries do not mean that you will be separated from the world. On the contrary, minimalism can be a way of reconnecting in a simpler and more holistic sense, without all of the noise and embellishments of modern society.

Think of minimalism like a small sandstone cottage in the middle of a small island in the middle of the great big ocean. Sure, you are separated from people and the world but bear with me. Your cottage is spacious and has everything you need inside it, nothing unnecessary, no clutter. It has been reduced to its essence and so have you. Everything that makes you unique has been actualized and you have the perfect little house to accompany you. Your house is simple and everything you need it to be; there is space and air and light. Now take this beautiful home you have created for yourself and within yourself and move it back into the world, into your country, into your neighborhood and place it right above your actual house. Minimalism does not mean you have to be stranded on an island in the middle of nowhere; it is a state of mind. Minimalism can exist in this chaotic world and it can bring you a sense of peace. Instead of blending into your surroundings, your home becomes a haven–you become a haven.

A crucial point to remember here is that positivity and peace can spread. By living a minimalist lifestyle you open yourself up to opportunities that otherwise would have been cluttered by the mundanity of life. Not only that, but a minimalist lifestyle equals minimalist waste. In a time of drastic climate change and environmental crisis, our loyalty to consumerism has failed us. Issues like fast fashion and landfills leave us constantly unsatisfied and wanting. Instant gratification fuels us and we attribute happiness to material wealth. Minimalism allows us to reject the plight of consumerism and planned obsolescence. It won't only help you, it will help the planet–and I think being conscious of your place and the influence you have on this world is a very noble gesture in times of mindless numbing. Feeling something becomes an act of resistance. But let's not be too hasty! The world will still be standing after you have finished the first few chapters and then we can focus on saving the planet. Right now, all I need you to do is sit back, relax and minimize.

Chapter 1: What *is* Minimalism?

Minimalism is, through the process of abstraction, stripping something down to its essential characteristics (Quote from O'Neill, 2017). Take a chair for instance. If you are looking at a gaudy, kitschy style chair with gold trimmings, pink floral fabric and an impressively opulent backboard that displays a wooden carving of all the Trojan wars and its victors; this chair has long not been a chair. It is technically a chair, sure—but it is also many other things and its true purpose has been buried underneath a grandiose display. Now, if we look at a chair that consists only of metal rods and a soft leather panel for you to sit on, we see no pretense, no falsity. *"This chair is a chair and nothing more!"* You would exclaim.

In a basic sense, minimalism is seeing something for what it is and using it for what it was intended. However, through the many years of interpretation, we also view minimalism as owning less. While minimalism is about owning less, this has sometimes been slightly exaggerated because people began viewing minimalism as an aesthetic rather than a philosophy. They would throw out their entire houses and buy fancy chairs and expensive cube ornaments and everything would be white. But the point of minimalism is not to go out and buy more! It is to make do with what you have and to make sure you are not living with unnecessary clutter. Minimalism assures you that everything around you is there for a reason and has a specific purpose. If it just exists to take up space then you must begin the process of letting go. This process may appear impersonal, but it is not the death of sentimentality, instead it allows us to cherish sentimentality. Minimalism creates space for all the things we forgot we loved and needed because we suppressed our desires with physical possessions.

By keeping all of your mementos and trinkets in a secluded drawer of your house, on top of another closet that you don't use, under a bag of old clothes– you are not doing them justice. You cannot just throw these treasures into a box and forget about them but still feel good about yourself because *you "kept them for all those years."* Keeping things does not show people how important they are to you. Keeping things creates a burden that blurs and stifles your true purpose (whatever that may be). As I said before, we are not going to be throwing your entire house out, but by creating space, you are allowing yourself to truly treasure your life and pay attention to matters that are important to you. You might find that you have extra time on your hands to learn a new skill, or get more work done, or simply practice mindfulness. This is because you are no longer holding onto objects that do not serve you. Your possessions will cease to weigh you down and you will be able to appreciate the present moment for what it is.

Minimalism is not just going to be a once-off sorting session. It requires constant attention and affirmation. You are going to sit with everything; your friends, your family, your work, your memories, and you are going to decide what your purpose is and what is important to you. We are going to strip you down like that gaudy chair until all we see is your frame, your true essence. And just how are we going to do that? By creating space.

Clutter means that our lives are already noisy and full and that can make it difficult to be mindful. Think of it like moving through a maze, except instead of luscious green hedges the walls are clutter and they are falling at your feet. Physically, it is difficult to walk through the maze. You may find things that distract you or require your attention, so as you move through the clutter-maze you take a few items. The lack of structure and sheer immensity of the clutter surrounding you leaves you feeling confused as you reach and grasp for more papers and possessions that you think you need. Eventually, you can no longer carry the weight of your possessions. That is what happens to your mind when it does not have space. You are unable to focus on one thing at a time and the clutter leaves you feeling overwhelmed and tired. By creating space, you can eliminate all of these negative emotions and streamline your way of thinking and how you move through your life. Space brings clarity.

Minimalism not only gives you space, but one of the main tenets of this philosophy is intentionality. To fully immerse yourself into minimalism, you have to be intentional with every single thing you do. This is why each person's minimalist journey is so personal and subjective because you have to decide what you need to be intentional about. And I don't mean being intentional with the breakfast you are going to eat tomorrow (although in the grander scheme of things it probably wouldn't hurt). I mean being truly and honestly intentional. Think about where you are placing your items, make sure everything has a home. Ask yourself why you want to buy that new dishwasher or if you really want to go out and see your middle school friend whom you have not spoken to in years. You need to look at your life and decide what you want, where you want to go, how you want to be and who you want to be. But don't be discouraged though, these are big questions and you are allowed to change your mind. Humans are constantly evolving and changing and that is one of the exciting parts about being human. You just need to make sure that at every moment in your life, you are doing what you want to do, and you are thinking about it, not just in passing, but really thinking about it. Strip everything down, abstract everything and find the true meaning, the true purpose, the true goal.

Minimalism is about taking back control of your life and not letting your possessions own you. To an artist, minimalism can be a form of rebellion. It is a stance against traditionalism and in a similar way today, we also use minimalism as a form of rebellion. We rebel against capitalism, against consumerism, against fast-food and fast fashion because they only provide us with short term satisfaction. Minimalism shows us that instant gratification and material wealth do not truly serve us and by implementing minimalism into our lives we are taking back control. *"No longer will I be a cog in this well-oiled machine,"* you protest, because minimalism allows you to take charge of your life and to create a space that you really, truly enjoy and appreciate. Whether your home is cluttered, your life is a mess or you just need some guidance–minimalism will give you the space you need to grow.

Minimalism teaches you how to let go. Not just of stuff, but of matters and people that no longer bring you pleasure. Why do you have three kettles, one of which is broken? Why do you have seven pairs of nearly identical jeans and why, for goodness sake, do you keep magazines from the 80s? Because you can't let go, because you are nostalgic. I can't blame you really, nostalgia is what fuels the human condition and sometimes all we have are memories. But you can't possibly hold onto every single one of them. Minimalism is the acceptance that life moves on, people move on, and we are not in control of that. While in some instances it can restore control, minimalism can also require you to relinquish control. As much as you want to hold on to that receipt from when you were in Paris five years ago; you simply can't. It serves no purpose to you and it keeps you stuck in the past.

Plus, if you want to hold onto that receipt or perhaps four of the seven pairs of jeans, then that's okay too! This journey is your journey. Sure, minimalism has some key principles that you need to follow but that does not mean that you can't put your own stamp on it. It is like a good pair of shoes, your feet have to be comfortable in them because you are going to be the one wearing them. Choose your own method, choose your own way, choose your own minimalism and remember that space equals freedom. Before I tell you how you are going to put all of that into practice, it is important to know how and why minimalism came about.

Minimalism Through The Ages

Minimalism through the ages has taken on many different shapes and forms and has come from many different places. Considering all of these varying interpretations allows minimalism to come into your home and heart as a comprehensive philosophy. One of the first examples of minimalism can be found in Japanese culture, in Zen Buddhism. Zen Buddhists explored minimalism through the processes of *wabi-sabi* and *ma*. Buddhist tradition often focuses on the concept of emptiness and material poverty as a means of spiritual enlightenment and wealth. For Zen Buddhists, separation from material possessions allows space for freedom and self-actualization. Zen also employs a holistic and timeless aspect to this philosophy as it recognizes that beauty dwindles, newness fades and our happiness cannot be dependent on these expiry dates. This is where the modern-day concept of minimalism and the ancient practice of Zen overlap. Both concepts are aware that having less can bring more and that the importance we place on worldly objects is fruitless.

Wabi-sabi, in a similar sense, speaks to intentionality. It embraces the raw quality of restrained beauty. Lauren Prusinski in her exploration of Japanese aesthetics uses the example of stepping stones. She states that with *wabi-sabi* the stepping stones are carefully and intentionally placed to look natural and imperfect. Instead of being reckless with the stones, one is cognizant of each and every stone's place in the arrangement. Nothing is pointless, nothing is wasted. In art, minimalism has often been about geometric shapes and symmetry, but Zen Buddhism embraces and praises the natural flow of life and beauty. Both philosophies expose the essence of something and allow it to be seen for its natural beauty and not clouded by the noise of trimmings and grandiose decorations.

Subsequently, the concept of *ma* pertains to emptiness and appreciating a space in its entirety. We are constantly trying to fill things up. Trying to fill up our bank accounts, our suitcases, our phones, our houses, but we forget that the absence of something can be just as powerful. By appreciating emptiness and empty space, we can focus. We know what the purpose of the space is and we know what it wants from us. There is no more guessing. *Ma* is not the aloof person you matched with on tinder, *ma* is intentional and wants to know you. By eliminating noise, waste and frivolity we create a space that we can interact with honestly and freely. The balance between user and object is refined and enhanced for a more comfortable experience because there is no more confusion about purpose or essence. In this way, these principles echo the simplicity of minimalism.

Similarly, Bauhaus' focus on functionality can be linked to these aspects of Zen Buddhism because they both function to eliminate noise and draw things towards their essence. After Zen Buddhism, the next mention of minimalism that historians can identify was in the 1920s. This most likely started with the establishment of the Bauhaus movement in Germany. Both the Bauhaus movement and the Zen Buddhist movement were in reaction to opulence and aimed to create a shift towards simplicity. Bauhaus was based on a few rigid principles which focused on form, functionality, good resources, smart design, technology and viewing the object as a complete work. The defining principle of the Bauhaus movement was its focus on functionality. People were tired of all the frills and superfluous details. They wanted to create objects and art with no historical origin, no story, no sentiment. By doing this, they adhered to one of the principle facets of minimalism; and that is to strip something down to its essence.

The Bauhaus movement also saw the use of geometric shapes (which is what later informed the minimalist art style) and primary colors as an ode to the abstraction of form and color. I lost you at abstraction, didn't I? Let's slow it down. Abstraction is an important part of minimalism because it is the process of removing parts of something to reveal and reduce it to its essence. Even after I've explained it, the concept still feels obtuse–*"but what is the essence of something?"* you're wondering. The essence of an object, for example, is its true purpose. What does this object do? Why do we use it? What purpose does it serve? By asking these questions we can understand that the object has a specific use and should, therefore, be made and used for that specific purpose. Think of it as an artichoke. You have to peel back leaf by leaf, layer by layer until you get to the delicious (and edible) part of the vegetable, the heart of the artichoke. Stripping something down to its essence is revealing its heart, the very thing that makes it what it is.

Figure 2: Bauhaus

As you can see in the above image, Bauhaus design is very practical. The colors are mostly prime or grayscale and the lines are clean. Form and functionality are of the utmost importance and these concepts are so clearly presented in the design of the couch and the lamp (even in the carpet!). The design is simple, clean and effective. There is no pretense, no need for excessive throws and cushions and adornments. In terms of minimalism, we can see that

23

everything has been placed with careful attention to detail, even the ornaments on the shelf have a specific order. In this way, Bauhaus depicts and takes as inspiration the intentionality of minimalism. The notion that everything has a place, a purpose and nothing is missing is evoked in the above image. Instead of clutter and embellishments, there is space.

After Bauhaus, minimalism reappeared in the 60s and 70s and never really left. It may not have been in the mainstream but it was always present and sought after. Minimalism in the 60s was heavily focused on art but interiors were also streamlined. If you can remember the cartoon *The Jetsons* which first aired in 1962 then you can kind of grasp the general aesthetic that people were opting for. They were looking for something modern, futuristic, clean and with that came minimalism. Sure, people went a little crazy with the colors and patterns but the furniture was practical and simple. The 60s was a time of technological innovation and we can see this influence by just looking at something like the washing machine. Similarly to Bauhaus' focus on technology and innovation, the washing machine provided a streamlined washing process that created space and reduced waste. I'm not saying washing machines were built with minimalism in mind, but they sure did add to the plausibility of implementing something like minimalism in the 60s.

In today's climate, minimalism is more prevalent than ever, as a trend and an environmental necessity. The overall appeal of minimalism in the 21st century is that it promotes functionality and streamlines work. You see advertisements and banners everywhere showing you how to decorate your office and home and almost all of them opt for simplicity.

Figure 3: Simple Office

We no longer require hanging pendulums and big bulky desks with thousands of drawers. What we want is efficiency. In a world that has so much going on and our being constantly available to people and information through our phones and laptops, we can't really afford any more distractions. This is why minimalism is back, and this time it is here to stay.

According to a prediction of modern trends that are here to stay, one of the most popular trends is using wood and concrete in its natural form. (This ties in nicely with the principles of minimalism because the wood has gone through a process of abstraction. To use these resources and materials in their purest form is to use them in their essence. In addition to this, the popularity of 'natural' furniture and plant-based decorations have been trends for the past few years and will most likely remain a trend. By natural furniture, I mean pieces that are made of wooden frames (bamboo is the new black).

Besides, people love having plants in their homes. This could be because city life is so far removed from nature and fresh air. I think one of the biggest reasons people obsess over plants is because they purify the air and can increase the amount of oxygen in a space. In today's world, with climate change and the sheer environmental destruction, being close to nature has become a priority. Apart from not only looking beautiful, they are also aligned with the philosophy of *wabi-sabi* because plants evoke nature's beauty. It increases and simplifies the flow of a space. Just remember to be intentional about your plant placement and make sure it honors nature and your space accordingly.

Figure 4: Intentional Plants

Minimalism as a Philosophy

So, minimalism in art is a little different. As I mentioned before, minimalism was a rebellion against traditional art. Not only that, but it was a criticism of art as a concept. By the 60s art had become an elitist and opulent market, leaving room only for the wealthiest and most influential audiences. However, people started to change their perceptions and the artistic community began to evolve. Essentially, minimalism was used to critique how people were engaging and interpreting art. The whole process was pretentious and people were getting lost in their opinions. This is because oftentimes a lot was going on, the painting or art piece addressed many different concepts and characteristics and audiences felt the need to consider the artist and the work as one. Conversations were inaccessible; so, academia and art became something forced and artificial. People were losing the essence and purpose of art.

Figure 5: Banana

For example, you might look at this picture of a banana on a pink background and wonder why? You would be right to do so. It feels random, perhaps even silly? Or you could go a different route and interpret it as a comment on the total destruction of meaning. The lack of bruises on the banana evokes the human desire for perfection, but the dark shadow behind it is indicative of our dark intentions, etc. Both could be correct, owing to postmodernism, but really it may just be a banana, right?

Kind of. With the rise of abstract art, Dada, reductionist art and minimalism, this protest soon began to gain traction and therefore meaning. But not in the way you would think. Remember how in Bauhaus they tried to create works without sentimentality and historical context? Well by doing that, the minimalists already made their point. Minimalists created art to be, in a sense, universal. For example, take an exhibition where the main art piece is a white cube in the center of a display room.

The cube has been reduced to its essence–it is a cube. But what makes it even more poignant is that no one can go to that cube and talk about the artist's possible relation to this cube, or the comment on how this cube is a metaphor for modern society because it just is what it is–a cube! By doing this, minimalists were saying: see things for what they are, without pretense, without pomp.

Although, before the 60s artists like Marcel Duchamp were also critiquing the state of art. Duchamp was more appropriately associated with the Dada movement, but the form of protest was similar and also categorically defined and inspired the minimalist movement in the 60s. Duchamp was quite controversial in his time because in 1917 he released a piece titled *"Fountain"* which was a sculpture of a urinal. Bizarre, I know–but not totally unfounded. Duchamp was commenting on the meaninglessness of interpretation. He wanted to display this sculpture of a urinal and watch people, with their pinkies in the air, say, *"Oh, this urinal is an ode to the society that we live in and the state of war."* When actually, all he was doing was testing the critics.

A more modern artist that also tested the opinions of his critics and viewers was Robert Morris, one of the founding fathers of the minimalist art movement. His most significant work was an untitled piece which consisted of several carefully placed mirrored cubes. His intention was shifted from creating a piece that had been abstracted to its essence, to a piece that confronts the viewer and calls them to consider their purpose and essence. This was a poignant piece because it focused more acutely on the user and their interaction with the art. This is aligned with the philosophy of minimalism because it portrays the inward consideration of your personal journey with minimalism.

Another influential artist at this time was Ellsworth Kelly. His work was somewhat aligned with the Bauhaus sentiment because he used bright primary colors and his strict attention to form could be found throughout his work. One of his most beautiful works, The Meschers, depicts the reflection of light off of a river in Paris. What makes this piece firstly, minimalist, and secondly, quite stark, is that it depicts the refraction of light with green rectangular shapes on a blue background. To the untrained eye, this may just look like a bunch of mismatched shapes on a canvas. What is so significant about this piece is that it uses both the philosophies of *wabi-sabi* and *ma* to create a piece that is evocative of nature (and the imperfection thereof) and emptiness. Kelly has abstracted the scene of light hitting the water to its bare and raw essence. The river can be many things, there could be a cloud in the reflection or perhaps a leaf floating atop the water or even a glimmer of all the little creatures floating beneath the surface. Kelly took one aspect, the light, and whittled it down until that's all it was and then he painted it.

I bet you're thinking, *"I came here to find out how to throw all my stuff away, why am I learning about art?"* Well, as I had mentioned before, minimalism is an all-encompassing experience and you won't only walk away from this book with a tidy house, but you will also walk away with a tidy heart and mind. To fully grasp the concept of minimalism and ensure that you do not relapse after you have thrown out all of your dearly beloved possessions, you have to understand it.

Chapter 2: Why Should You Declutter?

Right, now we are getting into the nitty-gritty part of minimalism. You know what it is, you know how it came about, you know that it's a way of life, but how do you implement that into your space? Why should you declutter? Well, in all honesty, there are many great reasons to declutter and I can't really think of a single reason not to declutter. Scientifically, it has been proven that living a clutter-free life can make you happier, healthier and more focused while living a cluttered life can lead to serious health complications like depression, anxiety and heart disease. So, why wouldn't you want to downsize and reduce the noise in your life? In this chapter, I will discuss how decluttering with minimalism can help you actively improve your current state of living and being. So, let's get to it!

Decluttering:

1. Increases self-esteem

One of the reasons you may find it difficult to declutter is because it can be a very intimidating process. When you look at your entire house you may begin to feel overwhelmed and question whether decluttering is even possible. I am here to tell you that it is and you can do it! When you do get to it, you will feel so much better about yourself. Obviously, if you set yourself the impossible task of decluttering the entire house in one day, then you will most likely feel bad about yourself and see it as a personal failure as opposed to an unrealistic goal.

If you declutter correctly, each item you toss away can feel like a victory and give you that extra boost of confidence you need to tackle the rest of the house. Many people suggest decluttering room by room or decluttering as you go, just let the decluttering wind take you. Processes vary from person to person and once you find a strategy that works for you, you will be flying through your house. Letting go will not always be easy and sometimes we can be sentimental and get attached to small things that serve us no real purpose. If those are things that are important to you, then you can keep them (to an extent, we are trying to be minimalists here, remember?). Often, finding the strength within yourself to cherish, thank and let go of these possessions can bring so much more joy into your life. The very act of letting go means that you are strong and with strength comes the confidence to continue. So, show yourself that you can do it! Give yourself the space and the time to grow and thrive.

2. Improves relationships

You wouldn't think that having clutter would affect your own life in such a way, never mind the people around you. Well, it's true. If you are not taking care of your space then how can you expect to be taking care of yourself and your relationships with other people. To be a good friend, spouse or parent you need to have the space and freedom to decide what you want and how you want to live. If you are unclear about this, then you risk putting the people around you into the category of matters that are cluttering your life and causing you anxiety.

In another sense, by creating a space that is so full of distractions and noise, it can be difficult for not only yourself to be expressive but also for other people. Say for instance you are married. You both work full time and are often exhausted when you get home. You drag yourself into the kitchen to put on a pot of noodles and ready-made pasta sauce for dinner. You slump over the chair in the kitchen and start checking your phone, mindlessly scrolling through other people's lives. Your spouse is sitting opposite you doing the same thing. This is your life in a cluttered environment. Now picture it without clutter:

You come home from a day of work in which you were focused and productive. You open the door to your house and it feels like you can breathe again because you created all of this space with the philosophies of *ma* and *wabi-sabi* at your heels. Your mind can finally unwind. You greet your spouse enthusiastically as they walk through the door and you move through to the kitchen to begin making a healthy meal. Your phones have been silenced, you no longer require the false sense of security that scrolling through your phone gave you. You have decluttered your home, your mind and your soul and you can now invite and welcome love into your heart. Downsizing your space means that you can give your relationships the attention they deserve. This is because, firstly, you are giving yourself what you deserve, and secondly, you have the space to do so.

3. Reduces anxiety

*"**How?**"* You might exclaim. We live in a fast-paced, high-strung society. We are stressed because we have too much to do, too many things to focus on, and not enough time. This way of life has allowed anxiety to creep into our lives like a thief in the night. Everyone is anxious, everyone is worried; *"how will I pay my rent next month?", "what if I lose my job because I double booked my schedule?", "what if the planet implodes because of climate change?"* These are all very pressing and heavy questions to be confronted with on a daily basis. The crushing weight of existence can often feel too heavy to even bear. And on top of that, your house is a mess, you don't know where half of your clothes are and you still have unread emails from three years ago. And now I have made you anxious just reading this!

Breathe. We live in complex and trying times, but minimalism can help you regain control. All of these things that are already causing you anxiety are only magnified by the clutter that surrounds you. By decluttering your home and your space, you also begin to declutter your heart. One of the key characteristics of anxiety is hyper-vigilance which causes you to be hyper-aware of every object, person, situation and potential situation around you. It can be exhausting and depleting. But as you begin your minimalist journey, you will notice that your way of thinking will begin to change. The process of letting go itself will allow you to not only let go of your possessions, but also the negative emotions attached to them, or yourself. By actively deciding to throw something away you can see it for what it is, or perhaps no longer is, and you can begin to part with it. Similarly, the process of intentionality forces your mind to focus on one thing at a time, and ensures that you do not get overwhelmed by your surroundings. Once the process of decluttering has come to an end, the presence of space will allow you to center other aspects of your life that you may have neglected while being consumed with clutter and anxiety. By creating a space in which you feel calm, focused and ready, you give yourself the opportunity to excel and relax.

4. Helps you focus

Not only on the tasks that you have to complete but because we are working with minimalism here, it will help you focus on all the aspects of your life that require attention. It will also help you center the things that you want to do. You have more time because you aren't constantly thinking about the mess that surrounds you. Similarly to how decluttering reduces anxiety by giving you a space to relax, decluttering helps you focus by just giving you space.

For example, say you are working from home and you have a pressing deadline that requires your immediate attention. You make yourself a cup of tea and a snack and you go to your desk to begin working. You take your laptop out and place it atop a messy stack of papers while reaching into your laptop bag for your charger. All you seem to find is air. *"Now where did I put that charger, I knew I saw it here somewhere!"* You ponder as you lift up the stacks of books and papers that surround you. You have several decorative toys stuffed in between the chaos of half-opened envelopes and sticky coffee stains. You get up to go and find your charger and almost an hour later you walk back to your desk proudly. *"Now I can start!"* You puff–but can you really? You open your laptop to a flurry of unread emails and notifications from your social media. Your computer reminds you of a memory you had this time last year and you sift through some of the other photos you took around that time. Another hour goes by and you have yet to begin working. You notice the table is sticky from your week-old coffee spills and you decide to clean it. You get sidetracked looking for a cloth and take another hour before you return to your seat.

I could go on like this forever, but the point of the analogy is that clutter is distracting. Not only that, but you probably missed your deadline. This can easily feel like a failure on your part and lead to feelings of depression and anxiety. Clutter takes your focus away and demands that you be at several places at once when you really do not need to be. Decluttering a place of work or a kitchen can enhance your experience by promoting streamlined and efficient task completion. It will not only allow you to focus but it will make it easier to maintain focus for longer periods making you more productive.

5. Increases productivity

This leads us to productivity. To be productive, you need to be focused, but productivity also relates to so much more than just focus. Productivity refers to the efficiency with which one completes tasks. Similarly to the analogy above, clutter has caused you to lose focus and due to this loss of focus, you were unable to complete the task required of you. This creates a snowball effect because being behind schedule makes it more difficult to center your attention on the task which in turn leads to decreased levels of productivity.

If you create a space in which there is little to no clutter, you can go to your desk, take out your laptop and charger and begin working almost immediately. You do not have to sort through stacks of papers and books, nor do you have to clean up coffee stains and take dirty mugs to the kitchen. You can focus wholly and freely on the task at hand and not be influenced or side-tracked by your surroundings. Minimalism ensures that you create a space in which you have room to think about things other than what is in the room. Objects are meant to serve a purpose, and when they no longer do that or detract from your purpose, then you do not have any more use for them.

6. It is better for the environment

"How can my tiny contribution to decluttering my home possibly help the environment?" Similarly to how your presence as a kind human can leave a positive impression on this world and the people in it, your actions can also have negative implications. It is our responsibility to make sure that we, as individuals, are doing the best and most we can to not only make our lives better but to make the planet a more livable place.

By adopting a minimalist lifestyle you are committing to leaving a smaller carbon footprint on this planet as well as being conscious of your waste. There are many options and ways to get rid of your possessions after you have decluttered. If your items are still in good condition you could even sell them! Save someone the trouble of going to the shops to buy a new toaster for double the price and sell them yours. If you do not want to sell, you can always donate your possessions which means that one less person is supporting consumerism. If you can't sell or donate your items, then remember the three Rs—Reduce, Reuse, Recycle. These are the principles that minimalism swears by, and coincidentally, so does environmentalism. Stick around and I'll show you some tips and tricks on just how to reduce, reuse and recycle so that you can leave a lighter mark on this planet.

How Does Living With Less Make You Happier?

I know this may sound crazy, but decluttering literally makes your brain happier. Studies have shown that people who live in cluttered environments have presented higher levels of cortisol (the stress hormone). Cortisol is usually released by your brain in response to a stressful situation or traumatic event. Cortisol tends to shut down your frontal lobe (the part of your brain that deals with rationality, reason and logic) to give your brain space to go into survival mode. Now, I'm not saying that people who live in cluttered homes are irrational and have no frontal lobe function, but what I am saying is that these higher levels of cortisol mean that your brain is constantly on edge.

Chronic exposure to clutter and high levels of cortisol also affect your body in the long run. High-stress levels can lead to depression, heart disease, memory loss (because high cortisol levels also shut down the hippocampus, where memory is stored) and anxiety. Basically, living in a cluttered space is also going to make you slightly unable to declutter if you are prone to symptoms of depression and anxiety. You might get caught up in a dark loop of clutter and depression but it is important to remember that you have to get up and try because decluttering will make you feel better. The happy chemicals produced from decluttering will force all of the negative hormones out of your body and you will soon be able to function as you once did.

If clutter can negatively affect your mood and stress levels, how does cleaning positively affect you? There has been some research on dopamine (the happiness hormone) suggesting that it is released not only when you do something good, like exercise or eat a healthy meal or go for a pottery lesson, but is also released when you anticipate doing those things. In the context of decluttering and minimalism, your brain is excited for the end result of all of your hard work, so even the act of slowly actualizing that goal (slowly cleaning room by room) prompts your brain to release dopamine at a consistent level. This is because you are excited! Think of it this way, remember when you were a kid and your mom said if you behaved that you could get an ice-cream at the end of the week? Oh, how you pined for that ice-cream! You went to sleep every night almost vibrating from excitement and you would wake up every morning and count the days left till Sunday. Sunday finally arrived and you got your bubblegum flavored ice-cream; two scoops and a cone. That night you lay in bed, full of sugar and happiness and quite content but no longer quite as happy. This is because the anticipation for the reward was perhaps even greater than the reward itself. I mean, the ice-cream was great but the whole event only lasted about five minutes. The dopamine was released when you were anticipating that ice-cream.

Not only does dopamine work in anticipation of a reward but it also brings in reinforcements in the shape of serotonin and adrenaline. Serotonin, contrary to dopamine, is a chemical and not a hormone and can, therefore, be supplemented into your diet (which is why you usually feel great after eating a healthy meal and exercising). Serotonin acts as a natural anti-depressant which basically means decluttering in an antidepressant. Now adrenaline, contrary to cortisol, plays a role in storing and 'saving' your memory. On the complete opposite side of the spectrum, decluttering can help you to focus by improving your recollection of information. The presence of adrenaline can increase your blood flow, help you sleep better and you know, not make you depressed or anxious. So, not only on a spiritual level will minimalism and downsizing help you, but also on a physiological level. Your brain is begging you to declutter!

On a more socio-economic tangent, living with less makes you happier because it means that you no longer abide by the rules of the rat race. Our lives are so integrated with consumerism and capitalism that it can be difficult to live without 'stuff.' Advertisements are constantly being shoved in your face telling you to buy the new phone, the new outfit, the new blender. Society is basically telling you to be unhappy and unsatisfied with what you have and is forcing you out the door to go and buy more of it! Minimalism as a philosophy teaches you how to be content and intentional with the things you have. By being intentional you are opening up a dialogue between yourself and your relationship with happiness. Do you derive your happiness from introspection and self-realization, or from external factors like other people's approval of you and material wealth?

You can ask yourself this: *"Do I really need this new phone because it has seven cameras and mine only has six?"* The answer is no. By being more intentional with what you already own and realizing that consumerism is basically the same as burning your money, you realize that you don't require all of these things to make you happy. I mean honestly, how long do you stay happy after you buy a new pair of shoes? You are probably super excited the first few times you wear them but after a few weeks you are onto the next pair. Instead of finding happiness within yourself, you create false and temporary happiness by buying and replacing things continuously. It's a vicious cycle. And no, I'm not saying you should never buy another thing ever again, but I am saying that you should not look to material items to bring you happiness.

Something that entraps you cannot possibly bring you happiness, and if it does, well then that's called Stockholm Syndrome. Minimalism provides you with the space and freedom to think about what is important to you. Space means that you can no longer numb yourself with clutter and freedom means that you can finally find true happiness inside yourself and your home.

Chapter 3: How Do You Make Minimalism Part of Your Life and Not Just Your Space?

It is not as challenging as one would think. Since minimalism requires intentionality and thought, it permeates its way into your life without you even realizing it. The whole point of clearing out your space is to create room for you to appreciate things as they are and to process emotions. By changing your space, you change yourself indirectly. As the Zen Buddhists practiced; emptiness promotes self-realization. This holistic interpretation of minimalism will be explored through the mind, body, soul and space in this chapter to show you how minimalism can not only change your space but your soul. You have heard the saying, *"when one door closes, another door opens."* Well, that is exactly what this chapter is going to consider. I am going to show you all the ways minimalism will guide you and open up your options by ending your relationship with clutter.

Mind, Body, Soul, and Space

Space

To start integrating minimalism into your life, you need to begin with the most tangible part of it, which is your space. It will be easier for you to begin looking inward and reaping the benefits of minimalism if you have the space to start thinking about these things. In the next chapter, I will be telling you all about the practical techniques of decluttering and minimalism, but for now, I want to explore the spiritual side. Remember that house on the island I was talking about? The one that became a haven for you? That is exactly what we are trying to do here. You have to decide what is important to you and how you want to interact with your space before you can start decluttering. Do you work from home? Maybe you like to create things in your spare time (like painting or pottery or gardening). Do you have children? Find out what you need from your space and let it serve you.

If you work from home, then you will probably need a home office. Make sure that your office is the first place you start. You will begin to see the changes where they matter most and this will spur you on to declutter the rest of your home. Clear out everything that does not need to be there. Make sure there are no distractions so that you can maintain focus and productivity and try to use pastel colors and white as your main color scheme. This will make the room look bigger and give your mind space to expand into all four corners of the room.

Do you have kids? Start with a room that you use for solace and relaxation. Make yourself a sanctuary before you color-code and alphabetize the kids' toys. Perhaps you are creative? I've got news for you, your studio does not have to be a mess. You don't need seven of the same kind of paintbrush and you certainly do not need three shovels in your gardening shed. Think of it this way, when your mind is running a thousand miles a minute, do you feel at peace? Do you have the capacity to think of new ideas? No, probably not. Your space is like your mind. If you have a million little pieces of paper and trinkets and pairs of socks surrounding you, then the chances that you are going to be able to focus or work are very slim. Prioritize your mind by assessing how a space makes you feel. Once you have figured out what in the room is causing your mind to spin, you can begin to address it.

By creating a space that allows you to breathe and be mindful, you are permitting yourself to follow that example. You are also showing yourself that it is indeed possible. While minimalism is about downsizing and owning less, it is also about how that makes you feel.

Mind

Figure 6: Clear Schedule

When was the last time you had an empty schedule? Probably when you were a very small child, and even then your parents had a timetable set out for you. Minimalism is not just about clearing out your space in a physical sense, it is also about clearing out other aspects of your life too. To do this you need to set up a game plan. Ask yourself:

- Why is my schedule so full?

- It may be full but is it fulfilling?
- If not, why do I feel the need to partake?

I use the example of your schedule in relation to how minimalism can benefit your mind because our lives are so busy these days. We have work, friends, family and many other commitments. That can be a lot of pressure. Have you ever just stood there and thought, *"I desperately do not want to go to this lunch date"*? Minimalism means trusting your gut. The fact that minimalism has so many different shapes and forms in so many different niches speaks to a part of the human condition. We crave simplicity and freedom. Being mindful about your time and space and how it affects you is not an unnatural concept, it just feels that way because we are constantly being pulled in all directions. Our minds are also heavily impacted by our schedules and the things we have to do. If we can separate ourselves from our commitments, we create a space for boundaries. Boundaries are like color-coded containers for your brain. Right now your mind is scattered and confused but once you start sorting your mind into categories and throwing out the ideas and thoughts that no longer serve you, you can regain control. Minimalism allows you to prioritize your life. Figuring out what is important to you is being intentional with your mind and what you let into it.

The most important question of the three that I have posed is whether your schedule is fulfilling or not. Sure, some things are unavoidable, but if your space is demanding less from you, then so will your schedule.

Consider your friends and family and how they make you feel. Maybe you don't have to stay in contact with the random person you met at a party last week? Freeing yourself from relationships and people who do not serve you is just as important as freeing yourself from possessions that do not serve you.

Body

Once your space and your mind have been decluttered, minimalism moves through to your body. As I explained in the previous chapter, decluttering has a positive impact on your brain. Apart from having to physically move to declutter (which totally counts as exercise), the increased levels of dopamine, serotonin and adrenaline promote blood flow. It also decreases the level of cortisol in your body which means that you will be able to concentrate and sleep better. Your body is able to function better in a place that understands its needs. This is also why minimalism has adopted the *wabi-sabi* philosophy with regards to plants and imperfect beauty. Being close to nature allows you to feel connected to the world and yourself. Plants give your body an extra boost to leave you feeling focused, energized and oxygenated.

Apart from the physical response your body can manifest in response to minimalism and decluttering, your body also undergoes a spiritual change. Minimalism inspires and opens the gates to mindfulness. This is the practice of being present. I know you might think you are always present and living in the moment but it is a lot harder than it sounds. We have so many things to focus on and most of the time we are either planning for the future or pining over the past. By being present, you acknowledge that you have no control over the past or the future, only of yourself in the present moment. Being present means being fully aware of your body and its place in the world, and accepting it as such. It is challenging to be mindful and present when you are surrounded by clutter, or are sandwiched in between appointments, or scrolling through your phone.

If you are going to give your body a fighting chance, then your space has to be aligned with your mind. Minimalism involves introspection and while I cannot tell you how to live, I can give you the tools, strength and motivation to make those decisions for yourself.

Soul

The soul has always been an elusive topic. No one can really define it. You can't see it or touch it. We do not know what it is. What we do know is that it is an integral part of our existence in this world. Basically, your soul is your essence. Just like that chair I described at the beginning of the book. Your soul is the part of you without all the trimmings, without the cute clothes, without the fancy technology. Your soul is what you are left with after you have stripped everything else away and only your true essence remains.

As I said, I can't tell you how this might look for you. People are different and they have contrasting purposes and varying priorities, so minimalism is not going to look the same for each person. The crucial take away from minimalism is that living with less can make you happier. At the end of the day, getting to know yourself without all of the embellishments and frills will help you grow and live a more comfortable life. This feels like a tall order, but the process comes about naturally as you address all of the other aspects of your life, like your space, mind and body.

You are also going to have to work at it because humans are constantly changing and evolving. Every day is going to be a new opportunity to abstract yourself and listen to your soul. Practicing mindfulness for just 15 minutes a day can help you to bring awareness into your soul. Remember to be patient with yourself and the process. Some days you will just want to go out and buy that new phone simply because it is new. If the connection and communication between your space, mind, body and soul is strong then you have nothing to fear. Giving yourself space through minimalism, both physically and mentally, connects you to your essence and allows you to experience the freedom of self-realization.

Digital Decluttering

"You want me to throw out half of my stuff, cleanse my mind, body and soul and stop me from using social media?" In all honesty, yes, but it's not what it sounds like! Minimalism is a philosophy, and if you are going to apply it to your home and your mind, then you should apply it everywhere. We spend hours scrolling mindlessly through social media, devouring likes as though they were sweet little cakes and drinking from the fountain of instant gratification as we receive all of the news around the clock. Minimalism can help you with your relationship with technology by promoting intentionality in your actions. By finding happiness from within and not as a result of external forces we can use social media to learn and benefit us, not stifle and pressure us. However, because it is so integrated with the present-day world, your job may require you to interact with these platforms on a daily basis and you are going to have to navigate how you want to approach it.

So what are some methods you can use to declutter your digital life? Well, for starters, as with every minimalist journey, you have to decide what you want from the process. You, through the process of abstraction, are going to strip down what social media and your phone mean to you and how they serve you.

For starters, you need to ask yourself why you use social media? What purpose does it serve in your life?

Do you like to gather inspiration, do you like to stay up-to-date with your family, do you mainly use social media for work? After you have figured out why it serves you, you can start to address your usage thereof. Perhaps you don't need to have so many apps on your phone. Think about the last time you used one of them and when you might make use of it again. If you are on the fence then you can live without it. What is useful about apps is that it is not exactly like throwing out your washing machine. You can't just go buy a new washing machine because you thought you wouldn't use your old one. However, with an app, you can delete and reinstall them at your own leisure. That does not mean you can go re-downloading apps left, right and center. Remember, to be intentional. Make sure that every app on your phone has a purpose that serves you. Sure, every app has a purpose, but if you aren't a photographer or a meteorologist, do you really need that random sundial app?

After you have downsized the space on your phone, you need to consider how you are using these platforms. Are you lazily scrolling through tons of images that don't necessarily influence you? Think of scrolling like fast-food. It sounds really tasty and it is relatively quick and easy, but as soon as you finish that double cheeseburger and fries, you feel bloated and full. While you may be briefly satiated, not even an hour later do you find your head in the fridge looking for a snack. That's the thing about instant gratification—it does not offer long-term satisfaction. Perhaps consider unfollowing certain accounts that you no longer relate to. Maybe you enjoyed them a few years ago, but you are different now and implementing minimalism into your life. Be intentional and cognizant of the kinds of people and information you are exposing yourself to.

"But what about work?" You ask. Well, some things you can't really control and can't help because it's your job and you made a commitment. It is also important to remember that very fact through. You made a commitment to work for a specified number of hours and that is what you are being paid for. You do not need to answer that email your boss sent you at 9 pm. You have dedicated two-thirds of your entire day to working and being available. Phones allow you to be connected and available 100% of the time when in actuality you aren't, and also don't have to be. This does not only apply to work but also to your family and friends. Because minimalism requires you to be intentional, you need to make sure that you have people in your life who truly serve you and who you are able to serve back. We get caught up in this thread of being constantly available even though sometimes we just want to throw our phones against the wall and not talk to anyone for at least a week. This is called being overwhelmed. Minimalism gives you space but you have to use it effectively if you are going to live a truly meaningful and happy life.

Another important way to digitally declutter is by organizing your files and photos. Everything is so easy these days and saving does not exactly mean anything anymore, it is merely a click away. So, why are you keeping that funny photo you sent your mom three years ago? And if you are truly adamant about saving it, why is it scattered in between your December family holiday photos and selfies? Be mindful of the content you keep and create categories that make it easy to find the information you are looking for.

Just as you would consider your physical space, you need to be aware that the same thing can happen to your digital space. Think of it as your house; one room is social media, one room is your emails, one room is your messaging app, one room is your files and the final room can be your photos. These are all things that can be sorted and organized. What is the use of having hundreds of files if you do not know what and why they are? Here is a small list that can help you organize your digital space, although in the next chapter, most of the tips and tricks I will give you to declutter your space can be applied digitally as well.

- Divide your files into categories.
- Make sure there are no duplicates.
- Use subcategories for organizational clarity.
- Ask yourself why you are keeping that file. Does it mean something to you? Will you use it in the future? If the answers to these questions are no then you should discard it.
- Consider the timeline. Having something recent on your phone or laptop is probably more valuable than having information from several years ago.

- Do not put everything *you "sort of"* don't use in a miscellaneous file. That's the same thing as clearing out your house only to stuff everything into a *"clutter closet."* The point here is to let go and find freedom in letting go and the space that it creates.
- If it does not benefit you, delete it.

This is not going to be easy, but I promise you it is going to be worth it. We have to move away from consumerism and the anxieties that it causes us and we have to distance ourselves from our constant desire for approval and instant gratification. In a world of fast-paced everything, we just need to slow down and breathe.

Chapter 4: How to Organize Your Space

Figure 7: Less

While minimalism offers more than just the prospects of a clean, open and livable space, we still need to focus on starting your journey to a fulfilled and realized life. We have covered the spiritual aspect of minimalism, but to truly reap the benefits, we have to start at square one: decluttering your space. In this chapter, I will help you choose a style of decluttering and minimalism that suits you. To thrive in your space, you need to accommodate your specific needs and context. There are methods for the list-makers of this world and for the nomads. I will also give you some tips and tricks for decluttering and reducing the noise in your life. Most of these decluttering strategies will bear similarities to one another but it is about choosing the best and most convenient method for your personal journey. Remember to take into consideration your personality, space, level of dedication and context when choosing a decluttering method because your choice could make or break you. In the event that you do choose the wrong method, there are strategies you can employ to get yourself back on track, but for now, here is a list of decluttering approaches:

1. **Track changes**

Goals, goals and more goals! If you are someone who loves a good list, then this is the method for you. Tracking the changes and progress of your decluttering journey is going to allow you to plan your next few moves and also see how far you have come. There are different levels to this, and depending on how list-obsessed you are, they do not all have to be employed.

You are going to be making a spreadsheet of the entire process. Start by making a list of all the rooms in your house. Then list all of the essential items in the respective rooms, but make sure that you are not physically in the room when making the list. This will allow you to get some separation from the items that you may want to keep (even though they might not be essential). List only what you need so that you can objectively move through the space and give yourself the opportunity to differentiate between what you need and what you want.

Once you have completed a spreadsheet of all of the rooms in your house and all the essential items within those rooms, you can begin to sort. Remove everything that you did not put on your list. No, you are not going to have to throw all of these items out, but it will give you an idea of how much clutter you are living with and how much of it is unnecessary. From here you can add a few more items to the 'essentials' list and get rid of the rest. Make sure to tick off every room that you have completed and keep track of the 'non-essentials' that you will be keeping. It is always nice to have a physical representation of the space so that you can see if you are making a dent in your clutter.

2. HIID

High-intensity interval decluttering (HIID) incorporates the same philosophy as the popular exercising trend known as HIIT (high-intensity interval training). Interval training is highly effective because it balances periods of high energy with periods of rest. Think of your decluttering as though you are doing reps. Instead of doing ten pushups, with 30 seconds of rest, ten sit-ups, 30 seconds of rest, etc. practice sorting two drawers, with 30 minutes of rest. This is very dependent on how much you want to sort, how much time you have and what kind of sections you want to organize. The point of this method is to get a lot done in a relatively short amount of time. Setting quick and easy goals for yourself will make decluttering fly by and keep your motivation level high.

3. Incremental sorting

Similarly to HIID, incremental sorting can also be compared to exercising. If you are training for a 15km run then you are not going to start practicing by going on a 15km run. The odds are you will be too unfit or too tired to run the whole distance. Instead, you start with a simple 2km run. Then you move up to a 5km run and so it continues until you have trained your body to complete 15km. It helps to think about decluttering this way because we often brush the exercise off as quick and easy, until you are halfway through and trudging through piles of old clothes. Decluttering is a marathon and not a sprint. It is going to take time and effort and you will probably have to train for it if you are going to be successful.

Start simple and set yourself an achievable goal. This goal can be anywhere from sorting one room by the end of the week to having the whole house sorted in two months. It is important to have something to work towards, otherwise you could get bogged down by the amount of work. Motivation is key. After you have set yourself a goal, it is time for a game plan. If you are going to declutter your bedroom by the end of the week, then you need to plan accordingly. Start small and slowly increase your load. An example of an incremental sorting schedule might look like this:

> **Day 1:** Start by deciding how many pairs of linens you need, which ones you don't like/need anymore, and which ones you want to keep.
>
> **Day 2:** Declutter your bedside tables, both of them.
>
> **Day 3:** Sort through miscellaneous objects, trinkets, photographs, anything non-essential to your bedroom space.
>
> **Day 4:** Tackle your closet (probably the biggest task of them all).
>
> **Day 5:** Bedroom sorted. Goal Achieved!

And you are done! You started small and slowly built yourself up to finish the race with flying colors. Creating a schedule for yourself can also help you focus on what you want from that space and what you need to do to get it.

4. The Becker method: room by room

This method of decluttering can be interpreted in a variety of different ways, so it is up to you to decide which strategy seems more logical or suited to your lifestyle. This method was designed by Joshua Becker and comes with a series of steps, mainly:

1. Set clear goals.
2. Make sure your family knows what you are doing.
3. Sort room by room.
4. Have fun and be aware of the benefits.
5. Look back at your goals (and maybe even change them).

Becker mentions that when sorting room by room it is important to start with the easiest room and progress from there. If you start in the most cluttered room you may be easily discouraged. Kitchens can often be a difficult place to start because we end up just throwing bowls, cups and utensils into drawers and cupboards. Pick a smaller, less cluttered room to start. The quicker you see results, the more motivated you will be when tackling those more challenging areas of your house. It is also positive to see your progress and show yourself that this is something you can and want to do.

This method is reminiscent of the incremental sorting method except it is slightly more rigorous. Each room needs to be finished before moving on to the next one. Sorting in increments allows some flexibility with goals, you can either decide to clean an entire room or just a drawer. The incremental method is more lenient and understanding of your context. If you work the whole day it can be quite difficult to be in the midst of sorting an important room like the kitchen.

Overall, the setting and revising of goals in the Becker method is effective and ensures that you stay on track and remember why you chose to become a minimalist. We know that humans are constantly changing and that we have to be continuously aware and intentional with our actions and thoughts. Being aware of how your goals change and how you want to move forward will show you how far you have come and how far you can still go.

5. Peter Walsh method

The Peter Walsh method requires time and some serious dedication. He divides his method into five simple steps:

1. Take everything out of the space.
2. Decide how you want the room to look.
3. Sort into 'yes' and 'no' piles.
4. Throw away or donate the items.
5. Complete step two with the 'yes' pile.

The reason this method needs time and dedication is because it requires you to empty entire rooms in order to re-envision and reorganize them. The idea of starting from a blank slate is attractive because we can often get caught up in specific layouts and structures once the furniture is already in the room. So, granted you have the time and energy, this is a great method to use if you are looking for a serious overhaul of your house.

6. Declutter as you go

This method is quite comfortable if you have a full-time job or a family and are constantly busy and running around. You do not need to declutter your house all at once. Minimalism is a process and you can do it at your own pace, as long as you remain intentional and motivated. Decluttering as you go means starting from where you feel comfortable. Perhaps that is at the start of the house, in the entrance, or maybe you are in desperate need of a sanctuary and would prefer to start with your bedroom or home office. If you don't really like making lists or writing your goals down or structuring your life to the letter, decluttering as you go will allow you to define minimalism for yourself. After all, minimalism is not only about the destination, but the journey and you may as well be in charge of how you actualize that.

Organizing Your Space

- **Start**

This might seem like a superfluous step, but you are probably reading this book because you are unsure of where to start. The best advice I can give you is to just go. Take the leap, throw away the first thing you see!

You are never going to find the perfect strategy or learn how to adapt these methods to suit you unless you try and test them. Don't worry if you are slow to start–we are all frequent visitors to the procrastination station. And the beauty of minimalism is, after you get going, the procrastination station becomes a distant stop on your train through life. As you eliminate distractions, starting is going to get easier and easier. Although, the Catch-22 is that you have to start if you want to reap the benefits.

It is kind of like when you have a big day ahead of you and you set your alarm for 07:20. You plan your day starting from that exact minute but there is only one problem; you hit the snooze button four times. Suddenly it's 08:00 and you are not only late, but you are frustrated and disappointed with yourself. Those 40 minutes of extra sleep are not even worth it anymore. You have to make a conscious decision to jump out of bed and run into the shower so that there's no going back. As I said, throw away the first thing you see because after that you will have started, and that is the hardest part.

- **Hierarchical organizing**

There are many ways that one can organize and there are many different hierarchies that one can use. I have found that the technique best suited to organizing for minimalism is the hierarchy of importance. Since you are not just throwing away a few things, it is important to make sure you know where everything stands in your life. Additionally, organizing things according to hierarchy is very useful when dealing with documents and paperwork. We all have a few drawers that we continuously shove papers into until we can't anymore, and then we find another drawer. By sorting your documents into degrees of importance you know what you have to keep and what you no longer require, like that coupon from the garden shop you still swear you are going to use. Well, I have news for you. That coupon expired years ago and you didn't even know it because it was lost in a drawer somewhere.

Start with indispensable documents (like birth certificates, banking documents and passports), you will never throw these out, they are here to stay. After you have put those aside, you can create another category to file documents that you have received in the last three to six months. You may need to refer back to these in the near future which is why it is important to keep them (these include banking statements, registration forms, and yes, maybe even coupons). The last category involves all documentation that is either invalid, expired, or advertising of some sort. You don't need to know about the special deal your mechanic was offering three years ago, chuck it out.

- **Timeline**

Joshua Fields Millburn and Ryan Nicodemus on their podcast *The Minimalists Podcast* explore the effectiveness of the 90/90 technique. They came up with a formula to help you decide what is no longer of any use to you. If you have not used the item for 90 days and do not see yourself using the item in the next 90 days, then you need to get rid of it.

This technique is so effective because it bypasses sentimentality and decision-making. The formula says no, so you have to throw it out. It is also adaptable to your lifestyle so you can either shorten or lengthen the time limit but three months is a good starting point. If you find yourself struggling with sentimental items or things you thought you might use, this method is the perfect trick to get you out of your head and to get your things into the bin.

- **When in doubt, clear it out!**

This is in a similar vein to the 90/90 rule because we often see potential in our possessions. I know you bought that beautiful dress to wear to a special occasion but have you worn it anywhere? *"But what if I have to go to a wedding or a classy event?"* You protest. You very well may have to attend one of these in the future but if you haven't worn the dress by now, the chances are you never will. By keeping that dress you are pinning the future of your happiness onto an inanimate object. Minimalism is about separating yourself from material wealth and the importance that we place on these disposable items.

It is like going to that party you didn't want to go to. Your friends convinced you but deep down you knew you wanted to stay at home and have some 'me' time. Remember every time your gut was yelling at you to stay home and you shushed it? Well, now's the time to listen. If you are in two minds about something, throw it out. If it truly served you and fulfilled its purpose, you would not be second-guessing it.

- **Differentiate between usefulness and sentimentality**

This, apart from starting, is probably one of the most challenging steps out there. It is so easy for us to get caught up in memories and nostalgia. Sometimes it feels as though without those objects, we might forget. The important thing to remember is that when one door closes, another door opens. Holding onto the past and items that represent your past can be more damaging than you could have ever expected. Holding on means that you have your feet in the past and your hands reaching out into the future. You are not fully invested in either and therefore put yourself in a kind of limbo. Being stuck in the past means that you cannot move forward.

I'm also not saying that you have to throw out every item that has some significance to you, but you need to be careful of what you do end up holding onto. Make sure these items will help carry you forward and not cause you to linger. Although, it is also not as simple as keeping everything useful to you and throwing out everything sentimental. You don't have to throw out all of your sentimental items and sometimes useful things can be problematic as well.

Unless you are an avid maker of apple pies or shoestring fries, I doubt that you need that high-end peeler (as an addition to the peelers that you already own). Sure it's useful, it has a purpose and it gets the job done, but is it useful to you? When in doubt, clear it out!

- **Label, label, label**

You might not be one for labels, and that's okay, but I am going to ask you to give it a try. By labeling your storage, you are setting up a dedicated space for your items. Labeling will help you to be intentional with your sorting and with the items that you end up keeping. If you just set up three boxes in any general direction and say that you want to put things in it, you will end up confusing yourself. You might throw some miscellaneous objects in there and in a month find yourself rummaging through the boxes to try and find that thing you chucked in and didn't give much thought to.

If you label your storage, you will avoid confusion and you will be able to keep track of the number of items you are keeping. For instance, if you have children, one of the boxes for your living room may be 'toys,' the other could be 'wires' and the third may be 'blankets.' Now you have a dedicated space for all of these items. You do not need to keep all seven blankets that you have (they won't fit into the box anyway), so maybe just keep two. What about wires?

Let's just toss them all in there and hope for the best, right? No. You are trying to simplify your life, not complicate it. Make sure you know what each wire is used for. If you don't know its purpose, you don't need it. Once you have figured out what the wires are for, wrap them up neatly, tie them individually and label them. Confusion will be a thing of the past and you won't lose things as often because everything has a place.

- **Everything has a place**

Which brings us to this point. Are you guilty of putting your keys in a different place every time you get home? Are you five minutes late to work every morning because you *"swear you left them on that table there"?* Intentionality requires consistency. You don't necessarily have to label every section of your home, it isn't a stationery store, but there are easier (and more visually pleasing) ways to organize your space. Put a small decorative bowl at the entrance of your house, or perhaps add a hook to the wall. Instead of throwing your keys around or leaving them in your jacket pocket, you can hang them up or keep them in the bowl. This method does not only apply to your house keys but can be a useful technique for things like jewelry, bottle openers, books and shoes. You can also consider using magnets to attach items to your wall or fridge so they are in plain sight. Just like you have a home, your things should have homes too. Think of all the time you might save because you no longer have to look for everything!

- **Digitize**

This pill may be hard to swallow because old photos are so sentimental and nostalgic and they really can't be replaced. Unfortunately, photos fade and they also take up a lot of space. Remember what I said about not placing importance on material objects and separating your happiness from them? Well, I meant it. If you are serious about living a minimalist lifestyle then this is a good way to practice letting go and remember that those memories are within you. Plus, it's not like you are throwing them away. The world is changing and it is much safer to store your pictures digitally than it is to store them in the physical realm. What if there was a fire? Perhaps ten years ago you might have run to your photo albums to protect them from the flames, but you don't have to do that anymore. Now you can focus on saving yourself.

- **Consider your context**

Figure 8: Kitchen

This is a useful tip for anyone starting their minimalist journey. Remember your context. If you are living alone, then you have no real need to have eight bowls, eight plates, twelve glasses (that all look different), or a fourteen piece cutlery set. In this case, we work from the 1+1 rule. You need one bowl, plus one extra. If you regularly entertain, then you need to consider what works for you on a daily basis, and when entertaining. Minimalism promotes having a neat and orderly space that embodies simplicity, and the same applies to your kitchen sink. If the rest of your house is a pristine example of minimalism but your sink is filled with endless dishes, then you are not doing it right. Having less cutlery means you will have to wash up more often and will, therefore, have less clutter build up. Consider your context, decide what you need to live comfortably and toss the rest.

- **Onwards and upwards**

We often think of our spaces in terms of the floor. We place all of our furniture on the floor, we move around on the floor, it makes sense. However, our spaces are three-dimensional and we need to start using them that way. Not all of your storage or shelf space has to be on the floor, think higher. Plants can hang from ceilings and bookcases can start in the middle of the wall. The possibilities are endless. Looking at your space in a creative way will allow you to create space in corners you never thought would be open. Vertical organization can play a crucial part in how you transform your space.

- **What happens next?**

Sometimes we get so caught up in the process of decluttering and throwing away that we forget to consider where our unwanted possessions are going to end up. Just as you are going to be intentional with your space and possessions, you have to be intentional with your waste as well. Is the item recyclable? If it is, then being proactive and finding your local recycling spot is a good place to start. Could this item help someone in need? Perhaps you have decided that you don't need ten winter coats. There are always people who need clothes, so contact your local shelter or charity shop. Lightening your load opens up the possibility to improve someone else's and in a world of cold, harsh realities, help is always appreciated.

Perhaps you are considering the usefulness of having a television. You never use it because you stream all of your favorite shows and watch them on your laptop. Streamline your process and commit to something you have already implicitly committed to. In this case, you might not want to donate or recycle a large and expensive item like a television, especially if it still works. There are so many marketplaces for you to sell your possessions quickly and efficiently. Sometimes recycling and being conscious of the mark that we leave on the planet can feel like an uphill battle, but once you get started the process becomes easier. It is hard to take on the world's problems by yourself but every little bit matters and your contribution is invaluable. Remember, the first step is always the hardest, after that you can look back on how far you have come and wonder why it took you so long!

Chapter 5: How to Stay Clutter-Free

You know how to declutter your life and space, it's time to figure out how to stay clutter-free. It might feel like after you have organized the entire house the job is done, you are officially a minimalist. You can go back to mindlessly wandering through life and buying yourself new items to replace the ones that you threw out. I hate to break it to you but unfortunately, that is not how minimalism works. Minimalism is going to require you to be intentional in everything you do.

Reading this before you have cleared out your house can make the process seem exhausting and probably the opposite of freeing. However, once you get cracking you will soon find that intentionality becomes easier with every step of the way. It just takes a few extra seconds to make sure you are putting something in the right place or making the right decision by purchasing a new item. Don't feel too bad if you relapse into your old cluttered ways. The chances are that it probably will happen, but to prevent that, here are some tips on staying clutter-free:

1. **Update your goals**

Remember that list of goals you made when you were picking a decluttering strategy? Unless your strategy was *"decluttering as you go"* then you definitely have a list of goals and you should take full advantage of it. First of all, it is motivating to see what you have accomplished. Your goals are points that can keep you energized and interested. Don't fall into the trap of keeping them the same, though. You need to update your goals consistently to ensure that you don't fall behind because you have *"achieved everything."* As you go through the process you will be able to identify what works for you, whether you can take on more or less and which goals were too unrealistic. Updating your goals means you won't fall into the clutter trap again because you will be excited and motivated to continue with your journey.

Don't stop at just updating your goals, upgrade them! As you move through the process of minimizing and downsizing you will learn more about yourself. To keep up with your exponential growth you have to set goals that will continue to challenge and motivate you. If your goals stay on the same level of difficulty then you might lose interest and decluttering will soon get boring and mundane. Keep challenging yourself and make sure you don't stagnate. A little tip to help you with your list of goals and level of motivation is to take before and after photos of your space. Living in a space means that we gradually see changes, but seeing a stark before and after photo can truly show you how far you have come and inspire you to keep going.

2. Reconsider it

We all go grocery shopping and end up buying double the amount of food we intended to buy. For this, I advise making a list before you go shopping and committing to it. But what about the other big-ticket items? Perhaps you are strolling through the snack aisle and suddenly come across a shelf of blenders and kettles. *"Oh, I have needed a new kettle for months,"* you start to convince yourself. Suddenly it is in your trolley and on its way home to meet its new friend, your other perfectly functioning kettle. Before you make this mistake, I have set up a list of questions that you can ask yourself to make sure you are making the right decision:

- Is it essential?
- How often will I use it?
- Why am I buying it?

Is it essential? If you do not buy this kettle today, will you be unable to efficiently boil water in your home? If the answer is no, then you can move on to the next question. If you can boil water without this new kettle, even though it is new and shiny and red, the odds are that you just like the kettle but don't necessarily need it.

Next question: how often will you use it? If you make tea every day then your answer will be often and you can move onto the next question. If you do not use the kettle often and already have a perfectly good one at home, then you do not need the kettle.

So we have gathered that the kettle is essential and will be used often, but why are you buying it? Are you buying it because it looks pretty and new? Perhaps it is on sale and you can get a good price for it? Is it better than the kettle you already have?

This list of questions is about justifying your purchase. I'm not saying that you have to go through this round of interrogation with every item that you buy, but if you are going to upgrade or replace something then this can be a good way to identify your intentions. A good rule of thumb is if it will take up space, you need to reconsider it.

3. Wait

Waiting is about restraint. This can be so challenging, especially when the 'SALE' signs are ushering you to the checkout desk. You have asked yourself all of the necessary questions and you need to make sure you answered those questions truthfully but you aren't completely out of the dark yet. Before you buy something, wait. I like to start with 30 days. If you can live without that item for 30 days then the chances are you do not need it. If you still need it in a month then you can reconsider.

You might find that waiting 30 days to buy an item is a bit too long and you would rather change your waiting period to ten days, or perhaps it is too short and you need 60 days. As long as you are taking the time to evaluate whether you need to purchase something new, or if your money is just burning a hole in your wallet.

Adjusting from a life of clutter can be difficult because we are so stuck in our ways. You might find yourself reaching towards your wallet, or itching to make that impulse buy and that is perfectly normal. Sometimes you wake up and all you want to do is buy something, that new phone, a cute jacket, but you have to remind yourself that in that moment, you are associating happiness with the prospect of a material purchase. Instead of growing in your space, you are relying on instant gratification to get you through the day. In this process, you will learn how to step away and gain the clarity you need to keep your space clutter-free.

4. Make a schedule

This step can be combined with how you manage your list of goals. Sure, everything in your house has a place but sometimes life can catch up with you. Making a schedule for yourself means that you can stay on track and not fall back into old cluttered habits. The timeline of your schedule is completely up to you. It could be a daily, weekly or monthly schedule but the point is that you need to keep track of your space and make sure all of your hard work hasn't gone down the drain.

If you are working on a daily schedule, it may include an hour of tidying, reorganizing or cleaning. This can be beneficial because, in the grander scheme of things, an hour is not that much time to dedicate to your space. You can view it as a time of mindfulness and meditation. Perhaps it is something you engage in before work, or after all of your tasks have been completed for the day. Sticking to a daily schedule as opposed to a monthly schedule can help you stay motivated and prevent a build-up of clutter.

If you opt for a weekly or monthly schedule then you need to have slightly more discipline because it can be difficult to get motivated after a whole month or week of slowly letting clutter build up. Making a schedule at the beginning of your journey also means that you can get yourself into a routine of tidying, organizing and putting things where they belong. Once you are in a routine it can be hard to break it.

5. Make sure it has a place

It can be challenging, in the beginning, to remember to put your keys in that little bowl next to the front door or to put your shoes in the cabinet. Intentionality comes with practice and similarly to how you made a list of goals and a schedule, you can make a mental note of where all of your items need to go. It can be easy to fall into old habits, but if you are going to stay clutter-free then it is going to take some effort from your side. It might sound like work, but view these steps as preventative measures. Wouldn't you rather put your seatbelt on, even though it requires a little effort, instead of not having your seatbelt on in the event of an accident? Decluttering is the same.

Making sure everything has a place is like putting a seatbelt on. If you are not intentional with your possessions then you may have to deal with the chaos of a cluttered situation again. It takes five minutes of effort for what could be days of reorganizing and decluttering.

6. Do it with a friend

If this is something you are considering implementing in your life, then the chances are that you have surrounded yourself with like minded people. Not only will practicing minimalism with a friend or family member make the process more fun and exciting but it will allow you to hold each other accountable. Perhaps you are competitive in spirit, turn it into a game and have some fun. Check-in on each other. It is also always great to have a second pair of eyes when decluttering. Your friend can act as a mediator between you and your possessions. They do not have the same attachments as you do when it comes to your clothes and furniture and can, therefore, help you make an objective decision. You don't have to go through this journey alone. If you are both dedicated then having moral support can help you stay on the journey to minimalism.

Managing a Relapse

So you really tried and despite your best efforts, you still came home to a desk full of papers and a sink full of dishes. I know this can be demotivating but it is normal to fall back into old habits. After all, humans are creatures of habit and it will take some time for you to get used to a new routine. There may also be other factors at play in your life. Perhaps you have children, or have experienced a personal loss, maybe things at work are chaotic. The main take away from relapsing is not to be too hard on yourself. We have to keep that self-esteem and motivation up and here are a few ways you can do that:

- **Don't feel discouraged**

Relapsing is part of the journey. How can you expect yourself to be a perfect minimalist on your first try? In any case, the perfect minimalist does not exist. Each person's journey is deeply personal and the sooner you realize that the sooner you will know that relapsing is not that big a deal. Allowing yourself to feel discouraged or annoyed at your purchases could easily plunge you into the depths of clutter that you worked so hard to rid yourself of.

We have all started our new year with a long list of resolutions that slowly dwindled to nothing by March. *"This year I will exercise and eat healthy,"* we proclaimed! Three months later we found ourselves rather un-victoriously eating a slice of chocolate cake in front of our favorite reality tv show. We have all done it. We have all set out to do something and failed. However, without fail, we commit ourselves to the same promise we have made for the last eight years. Failing does not mean you have to stop, it is just a small speed bump in your road to success.

Remember that not all failure is the same either. Don't be too hard on yourself for buying a pair of pants that you love. Sure, you didn't really need it and you could have asked yourself the three questions before purchasing the pants or even waited a week before committing, but it is not that monumental a failure. Forgive yourself and move on, otherwise minimalism will become a punishment instead of a gift.

- **Start small**

Okay, you have splurged a little. Your kitchen is full of shopping bags and nothing has a home anymore. How do you come back from this? Where do you even start? Do not fret, for the most heroic journeys have started from the smallest sacrifice. Start small. Just like how you started your journey to minimalism, pick up the first thing you see and start. It can feel like you are starting over and that all your progress has been for nothing, but that simply is not the truth.

You are not starting from scratch. Just because you had a small blip does not mean that you are back to square one. It might feel that way but you have to remind yourself that you are doing great. Pick a drawer in your house to organize or just put your keys back into their small bowl by the door. Pat yourself on the back and make a schedule to avoid falling back into your old habits.

- **Go back to basics**

Sometimes we just need to remind ourselves why we do things. Similarly to how you have to keep track of your goals, it is important to remember why you want to integrate minimalism into your life. What was your life like before you started clearing out your space, mind and soul? Did you feel fulfilled? Did you have time to focus on the things that you truly love? How was your mental health? You started your minimalist journey because you thought it would help you and looking back, it probably has. You just got lost somewhere along the way, so here is a quick crash course to minimalism:

1. Remember *wabi-sabi* and *ma*, the philosophies of imperfect beauty and emptiness. Even from the start, we knew your journey was not going

to be perfect, but that's what makes it beautiful and important.
2. Minimalism is about simplicity. It is about seeing things for what they are, in their essence. Once you see the essence of something, you must abstract your relationship with the item. Material wealth will not bring you long-term happiness.
3. Be intentional. Make sure that everything you do has a reason. Thinking about your process means that you are giving yourself and your possessions the credit they deserve. You no longer need to throw yourself into social gatherings and meetings that you do not want to attend or fill your house with objects that do not serve you. Being intentional with your time and space means that you value yourself.

Remember that minimalism is a long walk. Reminding yourself of why you are walking and where you are walking to, will give you the necessary strength to keep moving forward in your journey to fulfillment.

- **Ask for help**

If you are on your minimalist journey with a friend, then this step may be easier than you thought. The reason you are doing it together is to keep each other on the right track. Make a rule that you have to check with each other before purchasing something. Post daily words of encouragement to one another and make sure that you can both be a solid support structure for each other.

In the event that you are downsizing on your own, don't be scared to ask for help. You might even end up converting a few people! Sometimes people will surprise you and offer up some advice you never thought you needed. Perhaps you need to ask someone to check in on you from time to time or to help you declutter your closet. Just remember that you don't have to do this alone.

- **Be accountable**

This is one of the most important steps in your entire journey with minimalism, not just when you relapse. Have you ever had a friend who is dating someone and you know they are not right for each other? Try as you might, you can't make your friend understand that this relationship is not healthy or functional. That's because it is not your decision to make. You can hoot and holler all you like, but unless they decide for themselves, nothing will change. Minimalism works in a similar way. It has to be your decision. No one else can tell you what to do or how to do it. I can hold your hand through this book and guide you in the right direction, but you will continue to relapse if you do not hold yourself accountable and decide whether this is something that you want in your life.

Being accountable also means taking control and ownership of your life and space. It means that you are no longer at the mercy of consumerism and instant gratification because you have made a decision not to be. Being accountable can be a very powerful and motivating factor in your minimalist lifestyle. By forcing you to take responsibility it also gives you the power to make your own decisions and have confidence in them. This is something that you can carry with you even when you haven't relapsed. So, don't be discouraged! Be accountable, ask for help and go back to the basics, you will be glad you did.

Chapter 6: How Not to Do Minimalism

You know how to do minimalism right but how can you do it wrong? It's not really about right or wrong or how strictly you follow the guidelines. It's about whether you are using minimalism to benefit your life and how using it in a certain way can render these benefits either meaningful or meaningless. You are here because you want to downsize and reduce the noise in your life. To do this, certain guidelines should be followed, albeit you can follow them in a way that suits you and your lifestyle. The point is to change the way you currently live your life to be more fulfilling and wholesome. These 'don'ts' of minimalism will also help you stay on track and maintain your focus in what can be an overwhelming journey. This leads us to the first point:

Do not overwhelm yourself. You know all those "happiness" hormones we talked about in chapter 2? If you set unreasonably high goals then, unfortunately, all of those lovely little molecules that your brain worked so hard to create will just disappear and drop you further into a rut of cluttering. Setting unrealistic goals can be just as damaging as the clutter itself. Similarly to how you can begin to feel depressed and anxious because you are surrounded by clutter if you set an unrealistic goal, your brain perceives you not reaching that goal as a failure. If this does happen to you, set quick and achievable goals to get yourself back on track. Minimalism is about creating lightness, not adding weight.

Maybe you chose the wrong decluttering method and are finding your current approach too demanding and rigorous. Go back and choose one that suits your needs. While minimalism is going to benefit your life immensely, it can also be an adjustment and it is important to go as quickly or as slowly as you would like. Pretend you are in a relationship with minimalism. Maybe it is a whirlwind romance and you get married in the first month of knowing each other. Perhaps you need to take it slow and set some boundaries between yourself and minimalism. Whatever you decide, make sure you are enjoying yourself. Downsizing and owning less also means feeling less pressure. So, soak it up! Let minimalism wine and dine you.

My number two piece of advice is to give yourself time. Be kind to yourself, be patient and everything will fall into place. Minimalism is about the journey, not only the aesthetic of a tidy house. It is a process of letting go, being intentional and listening to what you want and need. So, don't put yourself in an awkward position where you resort to thinking, *"oh, well minimalism just isn't for me,"* because it totally can be. You just have to remember that you are a mere mortal and decluttering an entire house in a day is pretty much impossible. No matter what the guy from that home improvement show says. A lot of people start their journey with someone else's vision on their mind and this is where it tends to go wrong. It is easy to look at home decor magazines and wonder how you can achieve that same look, but unless you have a boatload of money and are an interior designer, your house probably won't look like that. Sure, you can find inspiration from looking at these magazines but your space needs to be a reflection of you. If it is a reflection of someone else then you will always feel like a stranger in your own home.

Tip number three: don't have too much stuff. I know this seems obvious but because you are new to incorporating minimalism into your life, it is a mistake a lot of first-timers make. You get caught up in the, *"I'll definitely still use this,"* or, *"what if I have guests over?"* trains of thought. While it is important to account for these possibilities, the chances that you host people on a weekly or even monthly basis are rather slim. If your life does include bountiful social gatherings and scheduled meetings in your living space then it is definitely important that you account for this when decluttering. Although, for those of us who do not engage in frequent social gatherings; we can no longer live and plan our lives with 'ifs' and 'buts.'

Realistically, you do not need an everyday set of plates and an incredibly expensive 20-piece set of fine china. Life is too short to wait for other people to eat out of your 'good' plates. Either use them yourself or sell them. When in doubt, clear it out! By being intentional with your possessions and your time you can successfully integrate minimalism into your lifestyle and home. Don't be fooled by potential.

I find that where people get snagged is when they start going through their closets and decorative pieces like pillows. It is not the 2000s anymore and you definitely don't need 20 pillows in varying sizes and patterns on top of your bed or couch. Don't worry, we all did it, but that does not mean we have to keep doing it. Minimalism is about simplicity and abstraction. Make sure that you keep the essence of the objects in your house and use them for their intended purpose. If a pillow is purely decorative then you probably do not need it. Another trap people often fall into is getting bogged down by gadgets. I know that tea steeper that looks like a bear resting on your mug is adorable but it is probably a little unnecessary. Remember to ask yourself those three golden questions.

Closets, on the other hand, are much more challenging because we have a certain attachment to the way we look and what we used to look like. One of the hardest and most crucial principles of minimalism is letting go. Sure those pants fit you three years ago, but do they fit you now? Remember, we can't live our lives through the lens of potential. If you do not wear it, donate it. If it is old or broken, repurpose it. You do not want to have a beautifully downsized home and then cry in front of your closet every morning because you have no idea what to wear. I know you bought that blouse in a quaint market while traveling through Thailand but you have not worn it in decades. Let it go.

Streamlining your closet means that you no longer have to spend hours deciding what to wear. Instead, you can spend that time learning a new skill, reading that book you never got to finish, or simply practicing mindfulness in your space. Don't get bogged down by indecision and clutter. It might be challenging but it will be worth it.

For argument sake, let's say you clear out your whole house, it looks amazing, everything has a place, there is so much space to feel and think, but as you turn into the hallway, you see a door. What could be in this door? You open it with curiosity. Well, if it isn't a room dedicated to all of the stuff you just threw out! This is a problematic way to do minimalism because you are not engaging with the process of letting go. The point is for you to create a space in which your material belongings can no longer weigh you down. If you just stuff them all into a hidden room or storage unit then those items still have power over you.

Similarly to how your closet will still plague you with indecision if you do not clear it out, that room at the end of the hall will do the same. What if you find that in a year's time you need something from in there? You wade through the clutter, the roomy is hazy with dust as you shine a flashlight over mountains of old clothes and broken toys. You aren't Indiana Jones and you certainly do not need to enter that room like you are in *Raiders of the Lost Ark*. Except unlike Mr. Jones, you don't find what you are looking for because the room is a disaster. Commit to minimalism and renounce your need for material wealth. Let go and reap the benefits.

Similarly, don't just apply minimalism to certain parts of your space, it works best if you integrate this philosophy into all aspects of your life. If you are going to make an effort to own fewer bowls, kitchenware and utensils, then make sure you do not leave them scattered on the counter. Minimalism is a conscious, intentional decision. You might have some days where you are just too busy to maintain your space or you might not be in the mood. That's okay. We all have those days, just don't let days turn into months. Remember to set a schedule for yourself and try and stick to it. If your kitchen looks anything like the picture below then you know exactly how you feel when it does. You can't focus on anything else. Even when you are working you find yourself planning your day around cleaning and dishes. Give yourself some peace of mind. Do the dishes as you finish using them, make sure everything has been put in its designated place and remember that it's okay to get stuck once in a while.

Figure 9: Scattered Dishes

Another way not to do minimalism is to put too much pressure on yourself. Minimalism is a journey to self-realization. Putting too much pressure on yourself defeats the purpose of the whole philosophy because it is supposed to give you space. You might end up replacing the pressures of consumerism and material wealth with the pressure of not having possessions. If this is the case, it is okay to slow down. The principles are there to guide and help you, not intimidate you into owning less.

Sometimes minimalist gurus can be very strict in their downsizing advice, for instance, some may give you a specific number of items that you can keep and tell you to throw everything else out. Some might set rules like, *"only one item is allowed on a tabletop surface."* This can be problematic because it means that you become fixated on the number of objects that you need to have as opposed to the freedom the space is supposed to grant you. People find that having a specific number can offer precise guidance in your minimalist journey but as I have said before, your journey is your own. Everyone has different requirements from their space and being confined to a specific number of items may result in feelings of anxiety and lower self-esteem because when you do not achieve that specific number you feel like you may be failing. If you want to have two vases on your living room table because they make you happy and you love flowers then you need to have the freedom to do that. The trick is that you need to be intentional in your actions and remember that less is more.

I know I said that you may have to digitize some photo albums and throw them out but that does not mean that you have to reject nostalgia and sentimentality completely. At the end of the day, memories and the things we have around us can make us happy and remind us of a day or time that we may have forgotten about. The important thing to remember here is that you do not derive your happiness solely from these objects because that can lead you down the rabbit hole of instant gratification and needless hoarding. If you are intentional with your sentimentality, just as you are with the rest of your life, then I don't see why you can't have a little bit of nostalgia in your space.

Is That Minimalism?

Now it is time for a fun game of, *"is that minimalism?"* We have covered how not to do minimalism but what about when you think you are doing minimalism but aren't? Don't worry, just because it is not minimalism, does not mean that you can't make it minimalism. You are halfway there now let's get you to the finish line! Question number one for our lucky contestant here on today's show *"Downsizing with Minimalism."*

If it looks like minimalism and smells like minimalism, is it minimalism?

No, it is not minimalism if you go out and buy a bunch of new things because they fit into the minimalist 'aesthetic.' Over the years minimalism has indeed become a widely sought after aesthetic in mainstream culture. However, while people are chasing white walls and sparse paintings they lose sight of the actual thought process and philosophy behind minimalism. One of the key points of minimalism is to own less. If you buy a few minimalist 'looking' couches and chairs then you have not really solved the problem. You still own too much. And if you throw out all of your old stuff to replace it with new stuff then the principle that calls you to separate your happiness from material wealth is null and void. The point of downsizing is to be happier with less, and you will be, but not if less is an aesthetic to you.

Is it minimalism if you have nothing left?

No, it is not minimalism if you clear out your entire house. Let's be honest, this is not exactly a realistic expectation to have when adopting minimalism. There are some things that you simply cannot function without, like a bed, or toilet paper or a toothbrush. Minimalism is not about depriving yourself to the point of discomfort or pain. It is supposed to make your life easier and create a space for self actualization, for you to fully become who you are, without distraction or clutter. You might be able to self-realize while sitting on your bare floor, staring at your bare wall, but what will you eat for dinner? Will you get a takeaway because you have nothing left to cook with? Are you truly helping the environment by fueling the fast-food industry?

When living a minimalist lifestyle it is necessary not to be too literal with your interpretation of the concept of owning less. Living with nothing is also a lot of pressure to put on yourself and as we discussed earlier in this chapter, minimalism is about releasing the pressure and expectations from your life. If you are going to live a happy and fulfilled life with less, then moderation is key. Start slow and work your way up to a space where you can embrace the emptiness of *ma* and the philosophy of minimalism.

Is it minimalism if you just do one room?

No, it is not minimalism if you declutter one room and not the rest. It's kind of like running one 5km race and telling everyone that you are a marathon runner. It just isn't realistic, or the truth. If you are going to call yourself a minimalist then you have to make sure that you are actively trying to live a minimalist lifestyle. This means, owning less, reducing your waste and being intentional. If you are only prepared to do this for a small portion of your space or life, then all you are doing is organizing.

If you want to fully integrate yourself into a minimalist lifestyle then it does not stop at decluttering your space. Remember that decluttering can happen in your social life, with the people you surround yourself with, on your phone and laptop, at work. To truly reap the benefits of minimalism and allow yourself to flourish, you have to welcome it with open arms.

Chapter 7: How Does Minimalism Help The Environment?

You're wondering what minimalism has to do with the environment, I know. The fact is that minimalism has everything to do with the environment and in a time where our planet's future may be at risk, it is important to consider the implications of our actions, as a human race. In this chapter, I will highlight how minimalism can change the world and how even your small effort can make an exponential difference. Once you understand that you have the power and influence to help, I'll give you some tips and tricks on living a more sustainable and responsible life.

It seems far-fetched but it is quite simple. If you own less, then you are buying less. It is kind of like being a vegetarian. You might not think that your single decision to not buy meat will impact the meat industry in any way, but the truth is that it does. Sometimes we look down on people who have turned vegetarianism into a trend but in reality, whether you are doing it for the right reasons or not, if enough people stop buying meat, the industry will decline and the environment will start correcting itself. If enough people stop buying meat, we don't need to worry about the dangerous levels of carbon monoxide in the atmosphere because we won't be breeding cows like there's no tomorrow. Overgrazing will become a less pertinent issue and we will save so much water.

Similarly, minimalism can have the same effect on the environment and society. By allowing minimalism to be widely practiced in the mainstream, we increase the positive effect it can have on the planet. The people who desire to own and waste less will no longer flock to stores to buy the latest clothing and gadgets. They will buy sustainably sourced food and reduce their intake of plastic. Over time, demand for these highly wasteful and seasonal items will decrease and because the market is diminished, a new, sustainable and waste-free industry can replace it. Instead of adding to the landfills, we can begin to address them and figure out ways to ethically and responsibly eliminate waste from our lives. So, I know you may think you are not making a difference, but your actions could inspire someone and before you know it we will be living in a world where people are in tune with their emotions and intentional with their actions.

The main point of this is to reduce waste, not only after you have decluttered, but while you are in the process of decluttering. That is why it is important to remain cognizant of the items you are discarding. Not everything has to go into a waste pile. Donating, repurposing and recycling are great alternatives to simply throwing things away. Do some research and contact your local charity shop or shelter. You won't only be helping yourself but you will be helping the people around you. Maybe you have some old books, CDs or DVDs that you no longer use. That would be a great opportunity to contact your local library or school and see if they could use those items. What about your old towels and linens? Perhaps you can learn a new skill and weave yourself a new bathroom mat? There are so many ways to repurpose items that you already have in a fun and exciting way. This also means that you don't have to visit the shops for new kitchen cloths or bathroom mats. You are saving money, reducing waste and learning a new skill! As I said, minimalism will benefit you in ways you never even imagined.

By benefiting you, it opens up a space for you to use your positive energy and experiences to benefit the people and world around you. Remember to source your goods locally. No, I don't mean buying dinner from the fast-food chain down the road. Just because it is in your neighborhood does not mean that it has been locally sourced or produced. I mean that you should go down to your greengrocer or a specialty shop and buy food from them. In all honesty, you don't really need to eat apples that have been imported from Spain or Iberian ham and you certainly don't need Venezuelan grapes (that is, unless you live in any of these places). Buying locally means that your goods did not have to travel halfway across the world to get to your doorstep.

In this way, you have already reduced the pollution caused by transporting these goods. Buying local also means that you are supporting smaller businesses that do not impact the environment as drastically as bigger companies do. By supporting local businesses you are reducing the amount of influence and control that large multinational companies have over mainstream culture and you are allowing your neighborhood grocer to thrive.

This is particularly relevant to the world of fast fashion. We, as consumers, are so used to following trends and having different styles dictated to us that we are constantly on the hunt for the next best thing. We fork out thousands of dollars just to fit into a certain aesthetic and to stay up to date with the latest styles and looks. And after you have bought yourself a beautiful black suede jacket with embroidered flowers on the breast and fringe hanging from the sleeves, they tell you *"that's so last season."* We constantly try to keep up and enter the race when the race has already been won. We do not stand a chance, but they still give us a participation medal and usher us on to the next trend.

While we're hopping from trend to trend, from summer to winter to spring, what happens to the clothes that are never sold? You got it! They end up in the trash. No, they are not given to goodwill or donated because that would not be profitable. The materials are not recycled or repurposed and they are not ethically or responsibly sourced. So, your closet just keeps getting fuller and fuller as you wait for the season when your black jacket will come back into fashion. The chances are it might still come back, but that could be in 30 years from now and by then, it probably does not even fit.

So, do not be fooled by the glittery prospects of being 'fashionable' and 'on-trend.' Instead, opt for a timeless look that leaves you feeling classy and dignified. This can be done by paying special attention to your wardrobe and the materials used to make your clothes. You do not need 20 pairs of pants and 30 different summer blouses because the reality is that you do not wear half of these items. Stick to a compact number of items in your closet that you can rotate between and mix and match for some variety. Stay away from synthetic fibers like polyester and nylon and opt for pure cotton, hemp or wool.

Sourcing your clothes from shops who use sustainable materials and craft them to last you a few years, and not just a season, will stop the industry from growing at light speed. If you adopt minimalism into your life then you will know that the fashion industry thrives off of your attachment to newness. Once you detach your happiness from the prospect of new clothes or material wealth, then you will be able to see the damage fast fashion has caused not only to the planet but to you. Fast fashion is the antithesis of being mindful as it requires you to always be thinking about the future and never allows you to be content with the present. If you enable and participate in these trends, you give up some of your autonomy and control. Minimalism tries to give some of this control back to you and in that, you find freedom; freedom from your possessions and the constant pressure to be new and better.

What Else Can You Do to Help?

There are so many ways that implementing minimalism into your life can help the environment. Merely the act of decluttering and committing to intentionality can already make a massive difference in how you view waste. It has become more important, and luckily easier, to be sustainable and responsible for the amount of waste that we create. By creating space through minimalism we can see why it is a significant part of our journey to self-realization. If you feel depressed or anxious in a cluttered and dirty environment, then you can only imagine how terrible the planet must be feeling right about now. It is time to make sure that we use minimalism, not only to improve our spaces and lives but also the lives around us. Let us show our support by engaging with some of these useful tips and tricks on how to make the planet a cleaner and more sustainable place.

One of the most widely known phrases of our generation: Reduce, reuse, recycle, has a lot more in common with minimalism than you would think. It can serve as a helpful guide on your minimalist journey. Reduce the amount of stuff you own, reuse items and recycle what no longer serves you. By reducing the number of possessions in your life, you in turn, reduce the amount that you are buying and therefore the amount of waste that you are collecting. If you buy a new phone, the waste you are amassing does not only stop at the package the phone came in.

First, we have to think about the production of this product. Were the materials ethically sourced? How much of these materials were discarded in the making of the phone? How was the phone packaged (does the packaging include an instruction manual, protective casing, and the box you buy it in)? How was the phone transported (was it shipped, flown, or driven to the shop)? When the phone arrived at the shop and you decided to buy it, was it placed in a bag? Did you receive a receipt? If you reduce the amount you buy, you reduce the amount of pollution that it takes to make just one single product.

Reusing and recycling are also important parts of the process, although not as effective as reducing your consumption. Certain materials cannot be recycled effectively and therefore contribute to landfills, but that does not mean that you should not recycle at every given opportunity. If it cannot be recycled, think of how you can use it to create something useful. For instance, plastic bags can be woven into colorful doormats. You could also repurpose a few of your items, like those bootleg jeans sitting in your closet.

Cut them above the knee and make yourself a pair of shorts. You can use the bottom half of the jeans as a dishrag or sew them into oven mitts. The possibilities really are endless and the planet will thank you.

Another way you can repurpose effectively is by using glass jars. We often buy perishable items that come in glass jars like peanut butter and pasta sauce and throw them away when we are done using them. Glass can be recycled quite easily and not only that, they make great storage containers. Take your jars with you when you go shopping so that instead of using plastic packaging you can fill those jars up and put them back in your pantry. You also don't have to lug around that plastic tub that has a strange red tint to it from all the lunches it's carried for you. Go recycle that plastic tub and convert to a plastic-free lifestyle. Glass jars are the perfect vehicle for your on-the-go lunch.

Figure 10: Glass Jars

Another great way to reduce waste is to stop buying plastic wrap, tin foil and paper towels. These fall under the category of single-use items and are a big problem for our environment. This is because they create so much more waste than items you can use several times. Think of straws and earbuds. One person can go through thousands in a single year. It is far more sustainable to buy yourself a metal straw and a silicone earbud that can last you for years. A great rule of thumb is if you can only use that item once, find an alternative. There are so many you might even find yourself being overwhelmed by choice. Struggling to find an alternative to plastic wrap? Try using beeswax cloth, you can even make your own! All you have to do is find those extra pieces of material lying around and dip them into beeswax. You can wrap your cheese, fruit, vegetables and leftovers in these handy little cloths and your food will stay fresh for days. Not only have you repurposed some of your material but you have also found a way to eliminate some plastic waste from your life.

Consider how you get around. Do you have a car, do you take the train, what about a bicycle? We often get stuck in our old ways of thinking and habits. "I know the bus route and this is the route I have always taken," you might say. But have you ever considered whether a bus journey a few blocks up the road is really worth it? Another factor to consider is that you now have a lot of extra time on your hands. In the past you were stuck choosing your outfit for the day and wading through piles of clutter, trying to finish a few dishes before you run off to work. Your life is simpler now and you do not have to rush around anymore. Maybe this is a good time to consider walking or riding a bicycle. Perhaps you live in a country where that is not exactly possible, carpooling is a great way to save money and reduce your carbon footprint.

Similarly to carpooling, you can buy items that have multiple uses. It does not make sense to have a wine opener, a bottle opener, and three different decanters for your wine. Instead, you can buy a wine and bottle opener and use only one decanter (perhaps the other two can be used as vases). Instead of having five different items, you can have three and come out feeling lighter and less cluttered. How does this help the environment you may be wondering? Well, instead of buying five different production processes and the pollution that comes with them, you only have to bear the consequences of three products and their respective pollution processes.

You know what you have to eliminate from your life, but what about adding things to your life? A fun way to bring yourself closer to nature is to have plants in your house. While having plants in your house may not actively be helping the environment, it will help your environment. Plants can contribute to the level of positivity in your space with their oxygenating properties and vibrant colors. Not only that but being close to nature will allow you to connect with it and make caring for the environment far easier and more joyous. It is easy to get angry with big companies that show no regard for the planet, but by doing your little bit and taking care of your piece of earth you can turn saving the planet into a positive and fun experience.

Lastly, one of the best and most important things you can do to help the environment by living a minimalist lifestyle is to take care of your possessions. Not attributing your happiness to material wealth does not mean that you see no value in material possessions, it just means that you are more intentional with that care. What is the use in clearing out your space, decluttering your life and then treating the objects around you as though they mean nothing? These objects work to serve you and fulfill their purpose, they are here to make your life simpler and easier and if you show little to no consideration for them, then the philosophy of minimalism is devoid of meaning. Clutter makes you lose sight of the things around you, but by being mindful and intentional, we can grow an appreciation for these items that we surround ourselves with.

Plus, if we take care of our possessions, we will be able to enjoy them for longer and not go out and buy new ones. Taking care of your items means you do not have to add them to the waste pile.

By owning less you are consciously committing to wasting less and while you may think your effort can't possibly make a difference, I have shown you that it can and will. By being intentional in the way you move through this world, you give yourself a chance to grow but you also give the world around you a chance to grow. Donating a few items may be difficult for you, but the very act could change someone's life. Maybe that jacket you gave away got someone a job interview. Maybe that medical book you donated to the school inspires someone to become a doctor. Remember, when one door closes another opens and if you send positivity into the roots of this world, it will thank you by growing.

Conclusion

So just to consolidate, let's make sure we understand the key principles of minimalism:

- Own less
- Create space
- Be intentional
- Reuse, reduce, recycle

These are the practical points of minimalism. They are essential to the success of minimalism as a philosophy because they create a space in which you can self-realize. These principles allow you to detach yourself from material wealth and focus on placing your energy into useful and fulfilling areas of your life. Owning less means that you are letting go of the notion that material items can bring you happiness. By letting go you are giving yourself the freedom to say no to things that no longer serve you.

Isn't it bizarre how the mere act of decluttering your space can bring on so many amazing changes in your life? Having the space and freedom to be who and what you are is going to blow your mind. You will find yourself walking through this world with lightness, literally and figuratively. You will no longer have to carry the baggage of the physical world, and you can throw out all of that emotional baggage while you're at it. We tend to hold on to things in life because we feel like we have to. We feel like we may forget about our high school experiences if we don't save those eleven trophies. Or perhaps that one day when our memory fails us, we will be able to look back at all of the stuff we collected and be reminded of our memories.

In reality, your physical possessions mean nothing. Your life has meaning because of the true human connections you make, not because you connect with material wealth. At the end of the day, your books, papers, shoes, clothes, trinkets and furniture are not going to help you if you are having a rough day. They aren't going to be there for you when you are sick or tired. Minimalism helps you realize that these things you cherish so dearly, are merely things and nothing more. Meaning is found in the essence of being.

Minimalism has come a long way, from its humble Zen Buddhist beginnings to its stark critique of traditional art. It started as a counter-culture and has come into the mainstream as a call to action. People chase after simplicity and space as they trudge through the claustrophobic streets of life. Our attention is demanded at every corner we round and from every person we meet and it becomes too much. Minimalism has stood the test of time and has come back stronger than ever because we crave to be released from the shackles of consumerism. By integrating minimalism into our lives we are saying no to waste, and no to falseness.

Today, we are faced with the overwhelmingly scary issue of climate change. As we try to maneuver our way through life we can get caught up in banality. We distract ourselves with endless loops of pictures and videos of people we don't know. We turn a blind eye to the planet as it screams out for help. Humanity has long been searching for a solution to these problems and perhaps minimalism won't be able to solve all of them, but it will definitely contribute to making this world a better and happier place to live in. Who wouldn't want to be a part of that?

After this book, you have got a lot of thinking to do. You are not only going to be cleaning your space, but you are going to be healing your mind, body and soul. You will also be saving the environment and making the world a simpler place to live in. You know how to implement minimalism into your home, life and soul and you are better for it! Don't worry if you relapse, you are only human and sometimes we just can't resist all the advertisements being thrown at us. You just have to remain focused and ask yourself:

- Do I need this?
- How will it impact my life?
- Can I live without it?

These are questions that only you can answer. Your success with minimalism will be solely based on your commitment to yourself and your happiness. Your journey is going to be very personal and unique to you. It is important not to get caught up in everyone else's version of minimalism. Some people like the pure white aesthetic and go to extra lengths to fit into it. This is not what minimalism stands for. Don't be intimidated by the rat race and don't fall victim to it either. Minimalism is a philosophy that holds intentionality at its core. As long as you are asking the right questions with regards to your space and heart then you don't need an uncomfortably square couch. You can keep your slightly round, fluffy couch, you can keep your patterned bedspread. You are allowed to still have things that you like, but it is essential that you do not derive your happiness from these possessions. You will have to consider what is important to you, in your space and in your life.

It's not going to be easy. Sometimes throwing something out is going to feel like a part of you is being ripped out. You have to decide if something is weighing you down or if it is giving you the space to lift yourself up. It may not always feel worth it, but if you trust the process then you will be rewarded. You will begin to grow. Think of yourself as a plant. When you first get it, it comes in a small little pot. As it starts to grow it needs a bit more space for its roots. If you keep watering it and keep putting it in the sun but leave it in that small cluttered pot, it will stop growing. If you move your plant to a bigger pot, it will get bigger because it has room to spread its roots into the soil. You are this plant. You can remain stagnant in your small comfortable pot of clutter, but don't expect to grow. If you give yourself the room to grow, then you will flourish into a big and beautiful individual with strong roots.

Remember to be intentional every step of the way. Check in with yourself. Make sure you are being patient with yourself and setting realistic goals. If temptation strikes, breathe through it and resist. We live in a world that sucks us into its worries and fears. You know how to take control and responsibility for yourself, you know how to say no to consumerism. Stay calm and confident in your ability to create a safe and healing space for yourself, without the noise and chaos around you.

Minimalism is about creating opportunity. By getting rid of all of the clutter and distractions around you a space is created in which you can truly live your best and happiest life. You have all the tools, now go out there and take heed of life! I have confidence in your ability to make this world a better place to live in, one day at a time, one item at a time. The environment will thank you, the people around you will thank you and most importantly, your soul will thank you. Welcome to the clean and calming world of minimalism.

References

Becker, J. (2019). What is minimalism? Becoming Minimalist.

    https://www.becomingminimalist.com/what-is-minimalism/

Becker, J. (2019). Stick to decluttering with the Becker method. [YouTube

    Video]. https://youtu.be/HIEpLLjswGY

Bench Accounting. (2015).Simple Office [Stock image]. Unsplash.

    https://unsplash.com/photos/nvzvOPQW0gc

Berndt, P. (2016). An Empty House [Stock image]. Unsplash.

    https://unsplash.com/photos/5i0Gn0TTjSE

Best, S. (2006). Minimalism, subjectivity, and aesthetics: rethinking the

    anti-aesthetic tradition in late-modern art. *Journal of Visual Art Practice, 5* (3), 127-142.

Delberghe, J. (2020). Bauhaus [Stock image]. Unsplash.

    https://unsplash.com/photos/r3mS96pW0vE

Deluvio, C. (2017). Kitchen [Stock image]. Unsplash.

> https://unsplash.com/photos/x108OZZfzdc

Dormer, M. (2016). Banana [Stock image]. Unsplash.

> https://unsplash.com/photos/sf_1ZDA1YFw

Eads, K. (2018). Intentional Plants [Stock image]. Unsplash.

> https://unsplash.com/photos/xRyL63AwZFE

Endres, D. (2020). A minimal-ish approach to decluttering. [Audio Podcast

> Episode]. Minimal-ish. https://podcasts.apple.com/za/podcast/a-minimal-ish-approach-to-decluttering-any-room/id1434905449?i=1000485746041

Goldberg, E. (2015). 5 powerful reasons to declutter your life. Goodnet.

> https://www.goodnet.org/articles/5-powerful-reasons-to-declutter-your-life-list

Harveston, K. (2018). Can the rising trend of minimalism help the

> environment. The Environmental Magazine. https://emagazine.com/can-the-rising-trend-of-minimalism-help-the-environment/

Kopanytsia, U. (2019). Glass Jars [Stock image]. Unsplash.

https://unsplash.com/photos/Exf1N6_UTZM

Lewis, J. (2020). Scattered Dishes [Stock image]. Unsplash.

https://unsplash.com/photos/bP7p8zRnb_s

Mackay, J. (2019). Digital minimalism 101: how to find focus and calm by

becoming a digital minimalist. RescueTime Blog. https://blog.rescuetime.com/digital-minimalism/

Millburn, J., Nicodemus, R., Banks, R. (2020). Owning Less. [Audio Podcast

Episode]. The Minimalists Podcast. https://podcasts.apple.com/za/podcast/owning-less/id1069757084?i=1000487771322

Mora, P. (2020). Interior design trends that will shape the next decade.

https://www.archdaily.com/945290/interior-design-trends-that-will-shape-the-next-decade

O'Neill, M. (2017). The history of minimalism. Ebay Collective Blog.

https://www.ebaycollectiveblog.com/articles/the-history-of-minimalism/

Slobodkin, L. (1986). The role of minimalism in art and science. *The American*

Naturalist, 127 (3), 257-265.

STIL. (2018).Clear Schedule [Stock image]. Unsplash.

    https://unsplash.com/photos/wtqe5nd5MYk

Sunday, J. (2019). Less [Stock image]. Unsplash.

    https://unsplash.com/photos/aA6z6hn-yro

VanEenoo, C. (2011). Minimalism in art and design: concept, influences,

    implications and perspectives. *Journal of Fine and Studio Art, 2* (1), 7-12.

Walsh, P. (2011). How to declutter any room in 5 easy steps.

    http://www.oprah.com/own-extreme-clutter-peter-walsh/how-to-declutter-any-room-in-5-easy-steps

Printed in Great Britain
by Amazon